The aircraft carrier INTREPID

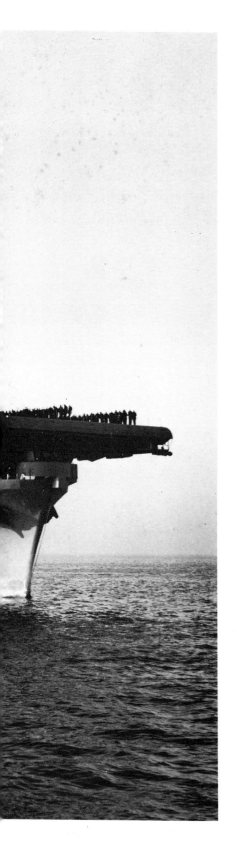

Anatomy of the Ship

The aircraft carrier INTREPID

by John Roberts

This book is published and distributed in the United States by the
NAVAL INSTITUTE PRESS
Annapolis, Maryland 21402

Conway Maritime Press

Frontispiece: *Intrepid* at Norfolk Navy Yard, 25 November 1943 showing the earliest modifications.

USN, by courtesy of A D Baker III

© John Roberts 1982
First published in Great Britain 1982 by
Conway Maritime Press Ltd
2 Nelson Road, Greenwich
London SE10 9JB

ISBN 0 85177 251 X

Designed by Geoff Hunt
Typesetting by Sunset Phototype, Barnet
Artwork by Letterspace, Barnet
Printed and bound in Great Britain by
Cambridge University Press

Contents

ACKNOWLEDGEMENTS

My particular thanks are due to Norman Friedman, without whose assistance in obtaining original material the production of the drawings in this book would have been very difficult; and to A D Baker III for kindly allowing me access to his collection of *Intrepid* photographs. I am also grateful for the help of N J M Campbell and D K Brown, RCNC in answering some of my queries.

PUBLISHED SOURCES

Friedman, Norman: *Ships' Data 7 — USS Yorktown* (Leeward Publications, Annapolis 1977. Co-authored by Arnold S Lott and Robert F Sumrall)
—— *Carrier Air Power* (Conway Maritime Press, Greenwich 1981)
—— *Naval Radar* (Conway Maritime Press, Greenwich 1981)
—— *Conway's All the World's Fighting Ships, 1922–46* (US Section. Conway Maritime Press, Greenwich 1980)
Green, William: *Fighters*, Vol 4 (Macdonald, London 1961)
Morison, Samuel Eliot: *History of United States Naval Operations in World War II*, Vol XII: Leyte (Oxford University Press, London 1958)
Rohwer, J and Hummelchen, G: *Chronology of the War at Sea, 1939–1945*, Vol 2 (Ian Allan, London 1974)
Sowinski, Larry: 'Champions of the Pacific: The Essex Class Carriers', articles in *Warship* Nos 5 and 6. (Conway Maritime Press, Greenwich 1978)
—— *United States Navy Camouflage of the WW2 Era*, Vol 2 (The Floating Drydock, Philadelphia 1977)
—— *USS Intrepid Album* (The Floating Drydock, Philadelphia, 1976)
—— *The Pacific War* (Conway Maritime Press, Greenwich 1981)
Thetford, Owen: *British Naval Aircraft since 1912* (Putnam, London 1962)
Terzibaschitsch, Stefan: *Aircraft Carriers of the US Navy* (Conway Maritime Press, Greenwich, 1980)

Introduction

Laid down as a fleet carrier in 1941, USS *Intrepid* (CV11) was one of a class of 24 vessels constructed during, and immediately after, the Second World War. As such she belongs to a remarkable group of ships – remarkable not for any great design innovation but for their proved effectiveness and reliability as warships and for the great size of the construction programmes of which they formed a part. In numbers of ships the *Essex* class was the largest class of fleet carriers ever constructed and as such could also claim to be the largest group of capital ships constructed during the steam age. The FY40 (Financial Year 1940) programme provided for 11, of which 5 – *Essex* (CV9), *Yorktown* (CV10), *Intrepid* (CV11), *Lexington* (CV16) and *Bunker Hill* (CV17) – were begun prior to the outbreak of war. The remaining 6, together with 2 more provided under FY41, and an additional 13 provided under the wartime FY42 (10 units) and FY43 (3 units) were laid down during the war. Of these ships no less than 17 had entered service by the end of the war while 7 were completed postwar and 2 cancelled. Another 6 ships were included in FY44 but these were subsequently cancelled and were never laid down.

The size of this class, and indeed the great size of the entire US war construction effort, not only reflected the enormous industrial capacity of the United States but also its ability to mastermind cooperative effort and the simplification of production requirements and methods. In other words, as might be expected from the country that produced the Ford motor car, it amounted to mass production. Early in the war it was decided to concentrate on the construction of existing warship designs, hence the *Essex* class represented the entire war production of fleet carriers. Another class, the *Midway*s, was begun in 1943 but none saw service during the war. Cruisers were largely represented by the 6in gun *Cleveland* class (of which no less than 52 were ordered) and the 8in *Baltimore* class, destroyers by the *Fletcher* and *Gearing* classes and so on. By concentrating on such designs building yards could streamline production, resulting in some remarkably short construction times. *Intrepid* herself was built in 20 months, while one *Essex*, the *Franklin* (CV13), was completed in just under 14 months.

This system was applied to material and equipment as well as ship design and a high degree of standardisation was adopted for such things as steel sections and plates, ship fittings, machinery and armaments. Production of AA weapons for example was almost entirely concentrated on the 5in/38, the 40mm Bofors and the 20mm Oerlikon – covering respectively the long, medium and close range defence requirements of the fleet. Naturally there are exceptions – mostly in the latter part of the war when, with the main construction requirements covered, US designers began developing the next generation of ships and equipment based on the lessons of the war.

The programme was not, of course, without cost – accepting existing designs as standard also meant accepting their basic limitations, of which the most troublesome was their overall size. The war resulted in many developments not envisaged when the ships were designed – the most obvious being the proliferation of radar and AA weapons which in turn required larger crews resulting in both substantially increased topweight and overcrowding of accommodation spaces. Consequently the *Essex* class, and practically all other US warship types, were by 1945 suffering from a substantial reduction in their level of stability and hence survivability in the event of damage. That this cost was acceptable in the circumstances is obvious from the success of the *Essex* class in operations against the Japanese during 1943–45, when they provided the main air strength and striking power of the Pacific Fleet.

CONCEPT

Prewar US design emphasised offensive over defensive qualities as had those of the Royal Navy prior to the First World War. However, whereas this had proved a less than successful policy in Britain's naval war against Germany it resulted, mainly by good judgement but partially by luck, in a close to ideal group of ships for the war against the Japanese. In aircraft carrier development this manifested itself in the provision of ships in which a large air group and its efficient operation took priority over passive defence. The logic behind this was that the aircraft were both the carrier's principal means of offensive and defence and if operated efficiently few if any enemy aircraft would reach the ship itself and even then they would have to penetrate the ship's AA barrage before they could inflict any damage. Thus the hull was provided with sufficient armour and water-tight subdivision to ensure survivability under all but the severest of circumstances but the remainder of the ship – that is everything above the main deck, which included her hangar and flight deck – were completely unprotected apart from the splinter plating applied to the bridge and gun positions.

The alternative system was that employed by the Royal Navy in the *Illustrious* class in which the flight deck and hangar were armoured but, on a given displacement, this degree of protection could only be achieved by a considerable sacrifice in the air group – US prewar doctrine required carriers with hangar accommodation for 72 aircraft, whereas the *Illustrious* class carried 36. It had its effect on carrier operation as well for while US carriers with their open hangars could start and warm up aircraft engines while they were still in the hangar, and thus speed up the rate of launch, this was not possible with a closed hangar.

Thus a large air group meant accepting the risk of a carrier being put out of action by damage to her flight deck or hangar. This proved a greater risk than imagined prewar, at which time it was assumed that any bomb hole in the comparatively light flight deck could easily be repaired aboard ship. This was in fact the case with some of the less severe instances of damage but it did not take account of the inherent vulnerability of the hangar contents – aircraft, their gasoline, and munitions – and in many cases US carriers suffered severely from fires and secondary explosion caused by a bomb or kamikaze hit. In this respect the kamikaze proved to be the most dangerous weapon used against the *Essex* class, although it was a form of attack that could not, of course, have been envisaged at the design stage. Being virtually a piloted bomb it stood a high chance of success but fortunately aircraft have poor penetrating power and thus were normally stopped by the flight deck – although their bombs, and occasionally their engines, penetrated to the hangar. *Intrepid* herself was hit by kamikazes on three occasions, two of which resulted in severe damage and her retirement from action for extensive repairs. However, the alternative to the *Essex* design, the following *Midway* class, which had a 3.5in armoured flight deck and to be fair many other improvements including a larger air complement, displaced 47,000 tons, nearly twice the tonnage of the previous class.

DESIGN

The *Essex* class design was an expansion of the previous *Yorktown* (CV5) class in which advantage was taken of the lapse of treaty restrictions and improvements in machinery design to enhance both aviation and defensive characteristics. Design requirements laid down in mid-1939 resulted in the acceptance of a design study for a ship of 26,000 tons standard displacement – 6000 tons above that of *Yorktown* and the largest of the outline designs proposed – in which the increased size was to be utilised to provide an armoured hangar deck, a larger flight deck, improved gun armament and increased aircraft complement. In fact the aircraft requirement was basically the same as in *Yorktown* – four squadrons of 18 aircraft – but to this was added a requirement for sufficient space for a reserve squadron together with a greatly increased spares capacity giving 25 per cent replacement parts. On entering service the reserve squadron actually became part of the standard air group giving the *Essex* class a regular complement of 90 aircraft against the *Yorktown*'s 72. Other improvements included provision for future (heavier) aircraft development – which effected,

TABLE 1: COMPARISON OF ESSEX AND YORKTOWN DESIGNS

Class	Yorktown	Essex
Standard Displacement (as built):	19,875 tons	27,200 tons
Length (pp):	770ft	820ft
Beam at wl:	83ft 3in	93ft
Aircraft capacity:	72	90
Main gun armament:	8–5in (8×1)	12–5in (4×2, 4×1)
Belt:	4in	4in
Main (hangar) deck:	0	2.5in
4th deck:	1.5in	1.5in
SHP:	120,000	150,000
Speed:	32.5kts	32.7kts
Fuel oil:	4360 tons	6160 tons
Endurance at 15kts:	12,000nm	20.000nm

hangar, elevator and catapult design, increased aviation fuel stowage (slightly more than that required as a result of the increased number of aircraft) and increased fuel oil stowage, the latter ultimately giving the *Essex* class an exceptional endurance of 20,000nm at 15kts – a considerable asset to both Pacific operations, in which great distances were automatically involved, and to aircraft carrier operations, which usually entailed deviation from the set course in order to turn into wind for the launch or recovery of aircraft and then regaining position at high speed.

Working out the design in detail together with some early additions, including an increase in the close range AA armament, raised the designed standard displacement to 27,100 tons and the full load to 33,000 tons.

MODIFICATIONS 1943-1945

Being among the first ships of the class to complete *Intrepid* followed closely the original design, from which later units were to vary in several details. Foremost among these was the bridge design, which in the first eight ships of the class included two Bofors mountings forward and in later ships only one, and the bow form which was extended forward in the later units of the class to provide positions for two instead of one Bofors mountings on the forecastle. Subsequently the early units had their bridge modified to the new standard but the bow, involving a major structural change, remained unaltered. It is worth mentioning that the long bow units also had shorter flight decks, these being reduced by 11ft forward and 7ft aft to give the bow and stern Bofors mountings clear arcs of fire. Overall length was of course increased (to 888ft) due to the increased overhang of the long bow and the stern sponson, whereas in the earlier units overall length was virtually the length of the flight deck including ramps and the slight extension of gun sponsons at the stern.

In detail *Intrepid* was modified as follows:
As commissioned: (a) carried 55–20mm Oerlikons, an additional 7 being accommodated in the platforms around the flight deck (by

reducing the spacing between mountings) and 2 more on the starboard side of the main deck aft, as compared with previously completed units. In addition the 4–20mm accommodated at the after end of the flight deck in earlier ships were moved to the starboard quarter of the flight deck. (b) carried 10–40mm mountings, 2 additional mountings being fitted on the starboard side of the main deck aft. (c) carried 4, instead of 5, as in earlier units, wireless masts along starboard side of flight deck – this being standard in later ships. (d) carried one flight deck catapult and one double hangar deck catapult (fitted only in *Yorktown, Intrepid, Hornet, Bunker Hill, Wasp* and *Franklin*). (e) fitted with SK radar antenna on masthead platform, SG radar antennas on topmast platform and at the head of a pole mast on port side of funnel, and SC radar antenna on starboard side of funnel.

November 1943: two additional 20mm mountings fitted on starboard side of bridge. SK antenna moved to starboard side of funnel, SC to pole mast on port side of funnel (SG in this position removed, presumably due to shortage as alternative position was available on the short pole mast at the rear of the funnel top). SM radar antenna fitted on masthead platform. Later, possibly at Pearl Harbor, the pole mast on the stack was increased in height and a YJ antenna fitted at its top.

March – June 1944 (refit at San Francisco): Forward 40mm mounting on bridge removed and bridge enlarged to occupy space made available. Three 40mm mountings added on starboard side below bridge, 2 on port side abreast flight deck and 2 on the port side of the hangar deck catapult sponson which was enlarged for the purpose. Mk 51 directors fitted for all new 40mm mountings. Hangar deck catapult removed and second flight deck catapult fitted on starboard side. Masthead platform extended aft to accommodate SK antenna and SC antenna moved to starboard side of funnel. Pole mast on port side of funnel replaced by IFF antenna bracket. YE antenna moved from abaft to forward of topmast platform to clear SK antenna. New pole mast with enlarged platform fitted at rear of funnel to carry second SG antenna and YJ antenna (latter subsequently removed). Windscreen added to screen forward of pilot house.

June – August 1944 (additional modifications at Pearl Harbor): Foremost starboard quarter 40mm mounting on main deck moved outboard to improve arc of fire. Upper signal yard added to topmast. Wind deflector fitted to screen around front of communication platform.

January – February 1945 (refit at San Francisco): Single 40mm mounting at stern replaced by two on extended sponson. Mk 4 radar for Mk 37 directors replaced by Mk 12/22. After starboard quarter 40mm mounting moved outboard to improve arc of fire.

May – July 1945 (refit at San Francisco): 19 single 20mm mountings replaced by twin 20mm mountings.

COLOUR SCHEMES

As completed *Intrepid* was painted in Measure 21 overall navy blue (actually blue-grey). During her refit of March – June 1944 she was provided with a dazzle pattern in Design 3A with the colours of

TABLE 2: **PARTICULARS OF USS INTREPID 1943—45**

Displacement:	27,100 tons standard, 33,000 tons full load (designed); 30,800 tons standard, 36,380 tons full load (as built)
Length:	820ft (pp), 870ft (oa)*; increased to 876ft 8in (oa) by 40mm sponson added at stern in 1945
Beam:	93ft (hull, max), 123ft (extreme, gallery deck), 147ft 6in (extreme, outer edge of deck edge elevator to starboard tip of signal yard)
Depth (moulded):	54ft 6in (main deck to keel), 63ft 1in (forecastle deck to keel) – no sheer
Draught:	23ft standard, 27ft 6in full load (as designed); 25ft 8in standard, 30ft full load (as built)
Immersion:	approx 110tons/inch
Machinery:	Four sets double reduction Westinghouse geared turbines; 150,000 = 32.7kts (designed), 32.73kts on trial at 32,346 tons; 8 Babcock and Wilcox 'Express' superheat boilers, working pressure 565psi at 850°F
Oil fuel capacity:	6160 tons
Endurance:	20,000nm/15kts
Electrical machinery:	4–1250kW turbo-generators, 2–250kW diesel generators
Protection:	4in Class 'B' belt on $\frac{3}{8}$in STS skin; $1\frac{1}{8}$in – $\frac{3}{8}$in STS side skin, belt to main deck; 4in Class 'B' bulkheads at ends of belt, $\frac{5}{8}$in STS bulkheads above; $1\frac{1}{2}$in STS 4th deck, above belt; $2\frac{1}{2}$in ($1\frac{1}{8}$in + $1\frac{1}{8}$in) STS main deck above belt; $2\frac{1}{2}$in ($1\frac{7}{8}$in + $\frac{5}{8}$in) STS deck, $1\frac{1}{4}$in STS walls in elevator pits; $1\frac{7}{8}$in STS holding bulkheads; $\frac{5}{8}$in STS longitudinal bulkheads (main to 4th deck); $\frac{5}{8}$in STS crowns and sides to magazines spaces and gasoline tanks; $4\frac{1}{2}$in Class 'B' sides, 4in Class 'B' bulkheads, $2\frac{1}{2}$in ($1\frac{1}{4}$ + $1\frac{1}{4}$) STS crown and $\frac{3}{4}$in STS floor to steering gear compartments; 1in, $1\frac{1}{2}$in and 2in (1 + 1) STS funnel uptakes; $\frac{3}{8}$in – 1in STS splinter protection to trunks, hoists, screens, bridges etc
Aircraft:	1943: 90 (36 fighters, 36 dive bombers, 18 torpedo bombers) 1945: 102 (6 fighters, 66 fighter bombers, 15 dive bombers, 15 torpedo bombers)
Flight deck:	862ft** (excluding 4ft ramps at each end) × 96ft (fore and aft), 109ft (amidships – excluding deck edge elevator)
Elevators:	One deck edge 60ft × 34ft 6in, two centreline 48ft × 44ft 3in
Catapults:	1943: one HIVA hangar catapult, one HIVC deck catapult; 1944: two HIVB deck catapults
Arrester gear:	16 wires (plus 13 wires forward for bow landings – removed 1944)
Barriers:	5 (plus 3 barriers forward for bow landings)
Gasoline stowage:	240,000 gal
Armament:	1943: 12–5in/38 Mk 12 (4×2 + 4×1), 40–40mm (10 × 4), 55–20mm (55×1) 1945: 12–5in/38 Mk 12 (4×2 + 4×1), 68–40mm (17×4), 76–20mm (38×1 + 19×2)
Fire-control gear:	2–Mk 37 directors for 5in (radar Mk 4 replaced by Mk 12/22 in 1945), 1–Mk 51 director for each 40mm mounting, 2–Mk 51 directors fitted for control of single 5in in 1944 (two 40mm Mk 51s on bridge also adapted to control twin 5in), Mk 14 gyro gunsights fitted to 20mm mountings c1944–45, 6–target designators Mk 3, 6–sky lookouts
Searchlights:	2–36in, 2–24in, 4–12in
Boats:	2–26ft motor whaleboats
Complement:	Ship: c2040 men, 130 officers Air: c730 men, 140 officers Flag: c130 men, 30 officers Total: 2900 men, 300 officers

Sister ships:
Essex (CV9), *Yorktown* (CV10), *Hornet* (CV12), *Franklin* (CV13), *Ticonderoga* (CV14)**, *Randolph* (CV15)**, *Lexington* (CV16), *Bunker Hill* (CV17), *Wasp* (CV18), *Hancock* (CV19)**, *Bennington* (CV20), *Boxer* (CV21)**, *Bon Homme Richard* (CV31), *Leyte* (CV32)**, *Kearsarge* (CV33)**, *Oriskany* (CV34)**, *Antietam* (CV36)**, *Princeton* (CV37)**, *Shangri La* (CV38)**, *Lake Champlain* (CV39)**, *Tarawa* (CV40)**, *Valley Forge* (CV45)**, *Philippine Sea* (CV47)**

* Units with 20mm AA platforms under after end of flight deck were 4ft longer (oa); the later long bow units were 888ft (oa)
** Long bow units had 844ft flight decks (excluding ramps)

Measure 32 (dull black, ocean grey and light grey – again these latter two actually contained blue, see dust jacket) which she carried until the end of the year. The same design was carried by *Hornet*, and with different colours by *Hancock* and *Franklin*. In her January – February 1945 refit she was repainted in Measure 12 – sea blue from the waterline to the main deck and ocean grey above, except for the masts which were haze grey.

Details of deck markings and colours are rather poorly documented. The flight deck was overall dark blue (deck blue) probably from completion and the ship numerals black. As built the deck stripes were light blue but these were probably changed to yellow before the end of 1943 and later to white. There were several possible variations in detail, two known to have been used in *Intrepid* being the outlining of the ship numeral in either white or yellow and the painting of false elevator markings to mislead kamikaze pilots – who were known to aim for these as they were weak spots in the flight deck.

GENERAL ARRANGEMENTS (see drawing section A)

The island bridge, like all carrier bridges, was cramped by the need to keep it to the minimum size. It contained principally the main command and navigating positions together with sea cabins for the senior bridge officers, a shelter for the flight deck crews and of course the boiler uptakes. Immediately below the flight deck the gallery deck – not actually a complete deck but a partial deck fitted under the deep supporting beams of the flight deck – provided most of the additional accommodation required close to the flight deck and bridge including the state rooms of the senior officers and the air crew ready rooms. Others areas were occupied largely by aviation and communication related workshops and stores. The areas under the flight deck open to the hangar were also employed as storage areas where such items as drop tanks and spare aircraft wings were hung from the deck head. Between the gallery and main decks the hangar occupied the majority of space, being kept as clear of intrusions as possible to maximise aircraft accommodation. Forward, the forecastle and the superstructure above it was employed largely for officers' staterooms while the other areas around the hangar, were mainly used as aircraft maintenance spaces although there were also some accommodation areas around the boiler uptakes on the starboard side.

Below the main deck the 2nd and 3rd decks were largely occupied by crew accommodation and spaces for associate services, such as the galleys. The original design provided berths for all members of the crew but the increased complement (resulting from the larger air complement, increased AA weapons and radar and other electronic equipment) resulted in the provision of hammocks for a large number of men. No doubt these were occupied by the newest recruits although perhaps some of the old navy men preferred such primitive sleeping arrangements. Access was provided fore and aft on the accommodation decks necessitating water-tight doors in the principal bulkheads which, although they would be kept closed in action, represented a danger to the ship's water-tight integrity. In later

designs these were abandoned, at the cost of convenient internal communication. Vertical access, to compartments lower in the ship, was better protected – the principal access points being via water-tight trunks designed to prevent the spread of flooding to compartments immediately above or below any area of damage. Below the 3rd deck virtually all access to the principal water-tight compartments was vertical.

The 4th deck consisted mainly of storage spaces including several large compartments for the stowage of aviation equipment and spare parts. There was also some additional accommodation space. Below the 4th deck the machinery compartments and the torpedo protection system occupied the majority of space. Sited fore and aft of the machinery spaces, on the platform decks and in the hold were those compartments requiring the maximum protection – ship and aircraft ordnance magazines, the gasoline tanks (one forward and one aft) the damage control HQ (on the 2nd platform), the main gyro room and the CIC (in the hold) together with various store rooms. Finally the triple bottom, together with the wing tanks of the torpedo protection system provided the storage areas for the main machinery's fuel oil and fresh water. Note that the drawings in section A show the ship as at the end of 1943.

HULL STRUCTURE AND PROTECTION (see drawing section B)

One of the most noteworthy things about *Intrepid*'s construction is its economical use of material, both in terms of reducing complications and in saving weight. Apart from the curves required in the outer bottom plating to produce the hull form and the camber of the weather decks, practically all structures are kept straight and flat. None of the decks have any sheer and even the torpedo bulkheads, although they follow the line of the hull, are made up in straight sections run as near parallel to the skin plating as possible. In addition the types of steel section employed were kept to a minimum, which obviously assisted the steel manufacturers to maintain adequate supplies. Apart from flat plates only 'I' bar and angle bar (in various sizes) was employed, other sections such as 'T' and '1' ('I' bar with one leg removed) being produced by machining the 'I' bars to suit, thus cutting an 'I' bar down the centre produced two 'T' sections. In addition the design employed a high level of welding – providing a saving in weight and time and improving water-tightness of joints. The outer bottom (or skin) plating except for the extreme bow and stern, the connections between the decks and the skin plating, the connections between the torpedo bulkheads and the 4th deck and the keel connections were of riveted construction but practically all the remainder of the hull structure was welded. (The butts of the outer bottom plating below and beyond the armour belt were also welded.) On a more detailed level some weight was also saved by machining lightening holes in deck beams and vertical girders, etc.

The hull proper (from the keel to the main deck) was constructed principally on the longitudinal system amidships and transversely at the ends, the main strength members being the keel, the main deck plating and the outer bottom plating adjacent to the keel (garboard strake) and the main deck (sheer strake). The keel, longitudinals, stringers, torpedo bulkheads and the main to 4th decks were continuous with the other structural members worked between them. Below the main deck the transverse bulkheads between the holding bulkheads were continuous with, at the ends, the platform decks worked between them. The emphasis on longitudinal strength resulted from the great length of the hull in relation to its depth (15:1) together with the high superstructure load – the entire hangar and flight deck. Transverse strength amidships particularly above the 4th deck relied heavily on the rigidity of the actual side and deck plating as the main deck beams were also longitudinal. Transverse supports were few – normally the principal transverse bulkheads with one or two vertical frames between them supporting the edges of a similar number of transverse beams under each deck.

The transverse frames or floors in the ship's bottom and torpedo protection compartments were spaced exactly 4ft apart being numbered from 0 at the forward perpendicular to 205 at the after perpendicular, each perpendicular being the junction of the ship's stem/stern with the waterline. (In the British and many other navies the after perpendicular is taken as the centre of the rudder post.) Those in the triple bottom were of three types – water-tight (fitted under water-tight bulkheads and at the boundaries of fuel tanks etc), solid non-tight, and open. The latter two types were placed alternately (in the section A drawings the open types – little more than transverse 'T's – are omitted to clarify the arrangement) except where local loading required the substitution of the solid type. Solid floors were also fitted at all stations adjacent to the keel and holding bulkheads for additional support, while the keel was still further supported by docking brackets spaced at half frame intervals (such intermediate positions were given $\frac{1}{2}$ frame numbers, ie $133\frac{1}{2}$, $134\frac{1}{2}$, etc). At the end of the ships, local stresses required a much higher degree of transverse strength and the frames were closely spaced at $\frac{1}{2}$ frame intervals.

The keel – a large 'I' girder built from flat plates with riders welded to top and bottom – and the longitudinals extended from the outer bottom to the third bottom, the inner bottom plates being fitted between them. The keel was water-tight but the longitudinals were non-tight except at the boundaries of the tanks in the inner bottom.

The underwater protection system was designed to withstand a warhead of 500lbs TNT and although this may not have been adequate to prevent the penetration of the holding bulkhead by many Japanese torpedoes it would, at the very least, have restricted the area of damage. The two outer compartments of the system were liquid loaded with oil fuel (replaced by sea water as the fuel was consumed) while the two inner spaces were void. Alternate compartments from outboard were framed in order to stiffen the bulkheads without risk of the impact of a torpedo explosion being transmitted directly to the holding bulkhead via the transverse structure, although this was of course a risk at the water-tight bulkheads which of necessity had to be

continuous. The holding bulkheads themselves and the main transverse water-tight bulkheads, were supported by vertical girders and horizontal 'T' stiffeners. A similar arrangement was adopted in the triple bottom as protection against ground mines and other under-the-bottom explosions, but this would have been of little value as defence against such detonations is close to impossible to achieve – although steps can be taken to minimise the effects of internal shock damage.

Armour protection was provided by Class 'B' armour and STS (Special Treatment Steel), both being nickel chrome steel alloys heat-treated to a uniform (homogenous) hardness and toughness. Class 'B' was used for thick sections – the armour belt and bulkheads – and constituted deadweight but the STS, manufactured only for thin sections, was, while retaining ballastic qualities close to those of full armour plate, an excellent structural material. It was therefore possible to save weight by making much of this plating both part of the structural strength of the ship and part of its armour protection. Thus the main deck, constructed of two thicknesses of $1\frac{1}{4}$in STS was both the upper strength member of the hull and its defence against bombs (being capable of keeping out general purpose bombs up to 1000lbs in weight). It would not of course have been able to stop a heavy armour-piercing bomb but it was considered that the fuze would probably be set off by the flight deck causing the bomb to detonate either before penetrating the main deck or very shortly after, in which case there was still the 4th deck, protected by $1\frac{1}{2}$in STS, to stop the splinters from entering the ship's vitals. However the ships were still vulnerable to AP bombs, either with long delay fuzes or through penetration of the hangar or hull side – it certainly was not a problem in the war against Japan but an *Essex* may well have suffered badly at the hands of the Luftwaffe whose heavy AP bombs came close to sinking the better protected *Illustrious* in 1941. STS was also used for combined hull strength and protection on the ship's side where the skin plating varied from $1\frac{1}{8}$in (sheer strake) to $\frac{3}{4}$in behind the belt; below this and fore and aft the hull was of standard medium steel. The structural qualities of STS can be judged from the fact that it was also used for structures not related to the protection of the ship, such as the keel.

The remaining principal protection was the $1\frac{1}{2}$in STS 4th deck, which contributed only slightly to hull strength as it was close to the ship's neutral axis, and the 4in Class 'B' belt and bulkheads. This was intended to provide protection against 6in gunfire in case of surface attack – principally a night or low visibility attack by enemy cruisers. Other protection consisted of an armoured box around the steering gear as protection against both shells and bombs, $\frac{5}{8}$in STS platform decks over the magazines fore and aft as an additional splinter barrier, and STS splinter protection to wiring, ammunition and access trunks, boiler uptakes, armament positions, radio and radar offices, and the principal command positions in the bridge. There was also a $\frac{5}{8}$in longitudinal splinter bulkhead between the 4th and main decks on each side (a continuation of the holding bulkhead below) closed by similar transverse bulkheads at the ends of the citadel. In all the protective system relied substantially on reducing the extent and effect of internal damage, which, combined with a high degree of water-tight subdivision and the US Navy's excellent damage control organisation, made it a great deal more comprehensive than would at first seem apparent.

The flight deck was supported by heavy vertical girder foundations, built above either bulkheads or side frames in the hull structure. These supported deep transverse girders or bents which in turn supported a few deep girders and several smaller 12in 'I' girders laid longitudinally under the flight deck. At the sides the spaces between the foundations were filled in with light plating except in those areas where roller steel curtains – for hangar ventilation – were fitted. The flight deck itself was of thin 0.2in steel plate with 3in thick wood planking laid transversely across it.

MACHINERY (see drawing section C)

The *Essex* class were the first US carriers to adopt a unit machinery arrangement, the machinery being split into two independent groups, fore and aft. Each consisted of two boiler rooms, containing two boilers each, and an engine room containing two sets of turbines. One pair of boilers supplied steam for one turbine set but a cross connection in the engine room allowed for alternative arrangements in case of damage or operating convenience. The turbines in the forward engine room drove the wing shafts and those in the after engine rooms the inner shafts. Fore and aft of these compartments were large auxiliary machinery rooms which, together with the auxiliaries in the main machinery compartments contained virtually all the ship's auxiliary equipment apart from the large equipments required for operating the aircraft elevators and catapults. The entire system proved very efficient, both in terms of fuel consumption and maintenance, largely a result of the US development of high power lightweight machinery over a number of years – a process not without cost as initially it meant accepting less than reliable power plants in order to solve the problems involved by practical experimentation. The details of the principal machinery fitted were as follows:

Boilers: The Babcock and Wilcox boilers supplied steam at a working pressure of 565psi and a temperature of 850°F. Both figures were substantially higher than in earlier machinery installations providing a higher power/weight ratio, and giving savings in weight and fuel consumption. It also allowed for a reduction in the size of the boiler uptakes, which helped to minimise the size of the openings in the protective decks, limited the encroachment of the funnels on hangar space and improved on the space available in the island superstructure.

The boilers operated under forced draught, each having two blowers (or fans) which fed pressurized air directly into the boiler casing (obviating the need for a closed stokehold) and thence to the air intakes around the oil fuel sprayers. The boiler had a split furnace – a standard saturated steam furnace on the right heating the main generator tubes connecting the water drum at bottom right to the steam drum at top centre, and a superheat furnace on the left to boost the steam in the superheater, at the boiler's centre rear, before its heat passed across to the saturated side to assist in heating the generator tubes prior to passing into the uptake. Further heat saving was achieved by an economiser fitted in the uptake, through which the boiler feed water was passed to be pre-heated by the waste furnace gases. Each boiler was supplied by a fuel oil service pump, a fuel oil heater, a main feed pump and, in case of breakdown or maintenance, an auxiliary feed pump. In addition there was one port fuel oil service pump, for use in transferring oil when ship power was off, and one fuel oil hand pump, for emergency use, in each boiler room. Separate fuel oil boost and transfer pumps and tank drain pumps were fitted in the after auxiliary machinery room, pump rooms and Nos 1 and 3 boiler rooms for the transfer, of oil fuel from tank to tank, etc.

Turbines: Each of the four sets of Westinghouse turbines consisted of a low pressure (LP) and a high pressure (HP) turbine driving the propeller shaft via a double reduction gearbox. The latter allowed a much greater speed reduction than the single reduction gearbox and again provided high economy as the turbines, running at a higher speed, were more efficient in their use of steam. The turbines were also of less weight but this was offset by the greater weight of the gearing. Astern turbines were fitted at the ends of the LP turbine (in the same casing) and a cruising turbine, for economy at low powers, was geared to the forward end of the HP turbine. When cruising steam was fed to the cruising turbine, then exhausted into the HP turbine which in turn exhausted into the LP turbine. At higher powers the steam was fed directly into the HP turbines. Each turbine set had a main condenser (slung under the LP turbine from whence it drew the exhausted steam), one motor- and one turbo- driven forced lubrication pump, a gland vapour exhauster and condenser; and for the condenser, a main circulating pump, one motor- and one turbo-driven condensate pump and a main air ejector. In addition each engine room had a lubricating oil purifier (or filter), a de-aerating tank for the feed water and four feed boost pumps to transfer feed water back to the boilers.

Electrical plant: Four 1250kW turbo-generators, located in the forward action machinery room, No 1 engine room and No 3 and 4 boiler rooms supplied the ship's main power requirements. Each generator had its own set of turbine auxiliaries, including a condenser, circulating pump, lubricating oil pump etc, as with the main turbines. In case of heavy loss of steam power two 250kW diesel generators were also provided, one in each auxiliary machinery room, each having a diesel fuel service pump, a cooling water pump and a fuel purifier. Ship's service motor generators, one in the forward auxiliary machinery room and one in No 4 boiler room supplied the majority of the ship's low power requirements. There were also three emergency 60kW generators on the main deck.

Distillation plant: This provided fresh water, for boiler feed and ship services (washing and drinking water etc), by boiling sea water and condensing the vapour. For economy of power the vapour generated from one evaporator was usually used to heat another evaporator before being condensed. The *Essex* class had three such plants, one small two-stage (or double effect) evaporator and its auxiliaries being fitted in No 3 boiler room, and two very large three-stage evaporator sets in the forward auxiliary machinery room. In each compartment two fresh water pumps were provided to transfer the distilled water to the ship's services and/or the feed tanks.

Air compressors: High pressure and a medium pressure air compressors were fitted in the two auxiliary machinery rooms and a high pressure and a low pressure air compressors in No 3 boiler room to supply air for armament, aircraft and sundry other purposes.

Degaussing system: As defence against magnetic mines the *Intrepid* carried an internal degaussing coil supplied by four motor generators, two in No 3 boiler room and two in the forward machinery room.

Fire pumps: For fire-fighting and wash deck purposes and for pumping out flooded compartments, nine fire pumps were fitted, one in each main machinery room, one in the after auxiliary machinery room and two in the pump rooms forward.

Bilge pumps: One bilge pump was fitted in each main machinery room for clearing the bilges and for pumping out the machinery compartments in case of flooding.

AIRCRAFT (see drawing section H)

As completed *Intrepid*'s air complement was 36–F6F fighters, 36–SBD dive bombers and 18–TBF/TBM torpedo bombers. As the war progressed the number of aircraft carried was gradually increased and the distribution of types changed to meet the requirements of the Pacific War. After her March – June 1944 refit she carried a preponderance of the new F4U Corsair fighter bombers – 65 out of a total air complement of 98. The remainder consisted of 8–F6F fighters, 10–TBMs, and 15–SB2C dive bombers. By early 1945 this number had been further increased to 102 aircraft (66–F4U, 6–F6F, 15–SB2C and 15–TBM).

As completed *Intrepid* carried an athwartships hangar deck catapult, at the expense of one of the two flight deck catapults originally specified in the design. Intended to provide direct launch from the hangar it proved less than useful in service and was removed in her first major refit, a second flight deck catapult being substituted. The cross deck catapult was fitted within a raised structure, as a slot could not be cut in the strength deck and was doubled – one track to port and one to starboard – for launching in either direction. To gain the required length a hinged extension was fitted to the outer end of each track.

Another feature quickly abandoned was the provision of arrester wires forward and crash barriers aft to enable aircraft to land over the bow with the ship going full astern. Again the additional equipment was removed during *Intrepid*'s first major refit, together with a second signal platform (for the LSO) fitted on the starboard side forward.

On the other hand the remaining aircraft equipment, with the exception of the gasoline system which proved vulnerable to ignition, functioned exceptionally well which, combined with sturdy aircraft and excellent training, gave the US Task Force carriers an enviable reputation for rapid launch, recovery and general aircraft handling. This was in part helped by two innovations in the *Essex* class: the deck edge elevator which, being beyond the main landing path, could be used when the flight deck was in operation with little risk of accident; and the increased area of flight deck resulting from the greater size of the ship and the adoption of an overhang on the port side (which maintained the full width of the flight deck abreast the island).

BOATS (see drawing section K)

As designed the *Essex* class were provided with a full peacetime complement of boats but no doubt due to the need to save space and weight the completed vessels carried only two 26ft motor whaleboats, one to port and one to starboard. These were carvel-built vessels powered by a 25hp 4cyl diesel giving a top speed of 7kts and had a maximum carrying capacity of 24 men each. Fully loaded they weighed about 4 tons. The principal lifesaving gear was provided by a profusion of liferafts and nets fitted under and around the gallery walkways and platforms. In harbour the ship would rely on the permanent boat pool for service craft.

INTREPID – CONSTRUCTION AND OPERATIONAL HISTORY

Note: For reasons of space this publication has concentrated on *Intrepid* during 1943-45 but for the sake of completeness the history below carries her story up to the present.

Builder: Newport News Shipbuilding and Drydock Co, Newport News, Virginia

Ordered: 3 July 1940

Laid down: 1 December 1941

Launched: 26 April 1943 (more properly 'floated' as she was built in dry dock)

Commissioned: 16 August 1943

September – December 1943: Trials and work-up prior to sailing for the Pacific via the Panama Canal

10 January 1944: Arrived Pearl Harbor to join TF58 (Task Force 58), becoming part of TG58.2 (Task Group 58.2) which also included the carriers *Essex* and *Cabot*.

29 January – 3 February 1944: TF58 provided support for landing on Kwajalein Atoll (31 January) by attacking Japanese bases in Marshall Islands. *Intrepid* with TG58.2 operating against Roi

17 February 1944: In preparation for landing on Eniwetok, TF58 launched air strikes against Truk. That evening *Intrepid* was hit in the stern during a Japanese torpedo bomber attack. Her steering wrecked, she retired to Majuro, under the escort of *Cabot*, 2 cruisers and 4 destroyers, where temporary repairs were carried out

26 February 1944: Drydocked at Pearl Harbor for repairs

March – June 1944: Refit at San Francisco

June – August 1944: At Pearl Harbor for training and work-up

August 1944: Joined TG38.2 (of TF38) which also included the carriers *Bunker Hill*, *Cabot* and *Independence*

28 August 1944: TF38 sailed from Eniwetok to carry out air strikes on Japanese bases in support of landings in Morotai and Palau

6 – 8 September 1944: TG38.2 attacks on Palau

9 – 10 September 1944: TG38.2 attacks on Mindanao

12 – 14 September 1944: TG38.2 attacks on Visayan (Philippines)

6 October 1944: TG38.2, now joined by carrier *Hancock*, sailed from Ultithi for operations off Formosa and Luzon

10 October 1944: Air strikes carried out against Japanese bases on Anami-O-Shima, Okinawa and Sakishima Gunto

12 – 13 October 1944: Air strikes carried out against Japanese bases on Formosa

15 October 1944: TF38 retired to prepare for assault on Philippines

18 October 1944: Air strikes against targets in Luzon

20 October 1944: TG38.2 provided air cover and strikes against Visayan Islands in support of Leyte landings

23 October 1944: TG38.2 took up position east of San Bernardino Strait to defend landing area against Japanese surface force approaching from west

24 October 1944: Battle of Sibuyan Sea. One of *Intrepid*'s aircraft was the first to locate Admiral Kurita's Centre Force at dawn. Subsequently the first air strike, from *Intrepid* and *Cabot*, achieved one torpedo hit on the cruiser *Myoko* and one torpedo and one bomb hit on the battleship *Musashi*. The second wave, from the same ships, achieved a further torpedo hit and four bomb hits on *Musashi*. *Intrepid* did not contribute to the next strikes but in the final attack her aircraft together with those of *Cabot*, *Enterprise*, *Essex* and *Franklin* achieved several torpedo and bomb hits on *Musashi* which subsequently sank. The remainder of the Japanese force turned about and retired

25 October 1944: Battle of Cape Engano. Together with the other carriers of TF38 contributed to the destruction of the Japanese Northern (feint) attack force, in which the carriers *Zuiho*, *Chitose*, *Chiyoda* and *Zuikaku* were sunk

28 October 1944: Returned to providing air strikes for Leyte landing area

29 October 1944: *Intrepid* hit by kamikaze – damage slight but 10 killed and 6 wounded

30 October 1944: TF38 retired to Ulithi

2 November 1944: TG38.2 arrived Utithi but quickly recalled for operations against Luzon

5 – 25 November 1944: Air strikes against Luzon interspersed with replenishment at sea

25 November 1944: *Intrepid* hit by two kamikazes, one abreast after end of bridge, one slightly further aft. Bomb from second detonated in the gallery deck starting fires which were extinguished two hours later. Casualties were 69 dead and 35 injured, while the ship herself was seriously damaged, and unable to continue flight operations

27 November 1944: *Intrepid* arrived Ulithi and subsequently sailed for Pearl Harbor on route for the East Coast for refit and repair

January – February 1945: Refit at San Francisco

13 March 1945: Arrived Ulithi to join TG58.4 (TF58) which also included the carriers *Yorktown*, *Langley* and *Independence*

14 March 1945: TF58 sailed from Ulithi for operations against Japanese mainland

18 March 1945: *Intrepid* near-missed by kamikaze which caused minor fires

18 – 19 March 1945: Air strikes against Kyushu, Kure and bases in the Inland Sea

23 – 25 March 1945: Air strikes against Okinawa in preparation for landings (1 April)

8 – 16 April 1945: Maintining cycle of air strike/replenishment while covering Okinawa beachhead

16 April 1945: *Intrepid* hit by kamikaze and seriously damaged – hangar set on fire but extinguished, casualties 8 killed and 21 wounded. She was able to recover her aircraft but had to retire to Ulithi for temporary repairs prior to sailing to the East Coast via Pearl Harbor for refit

May – July 1945: Refit and repair at San Francisco

July 1945: *Intrepid* joined TG38.2 which also included the carriers *Randolph*, *Antietam* and *Cabot*

6 August 1945: Air strike against Wake

25 August 1945: TF38 provided air cover for police duty over Japanese mainland and surrounding waters
5 September – 11 October 1945: *Intrepid* with *Antietam* and *Cabot* (TF72) provided air cover for reoccupation of Korea
11 October 1945: *Intrepid* relieved by carrier *Boxer* and sailed home
1946: Operating in home waters
22 March 1947: Placed in reserve
February 1952: Reactivated for modernisation under SCB-27C
October 1954: Recommissioned
1954-56: East Coast and Mediterranean
1956 – May 1957: Modernisation under SCB-125
1957 – 1965: East Coast and Mediterranean
1962: Reclassified as anti-submarine carrier (CVS)
April – October 1965: FRAM II modernisation at New York NYd
1966-68: Based on East Coast with three periods of duty off Vietnam – 6 months in 1966 and 3½ months each in 1967 and 1968
1968-1974: East Coast and Mediterranean
March 1974: Decommissioned and placed in reserve
1978: Plans were set in train to preserve the *Intrepid* as an aerospace and naval museum at New York. These plans are now (1982) well under way

TABLE 3: **PARTICULARS OF AIRCRAFT**

GRUMMAN F6F–3 'HELLCAT'

Type:	Single seat fighter
Date of entering service:	1943 (carried by *Intrepid* throughout war service)
Wingspan:	42ft 10in (16ft 2in folded)
Wing area:	334 sq ft
Length:	33ft 7in
Weight:	9042lbs (net), 11,380lbs (normal load)
Speed:	335mph at sea level, 375mph at 17,300ft
Engine:	2000hp, 18cyl, Pratt and Whitney R2800-10
Fuel capacity:	144 gal
Range:	1090 miles (normal) at 160mph, 1590 miles with 125 gal drop tank
Ceiling:	38,400ft
Armament:	6–0.50cal MG (400rpg) plus alternative loads of 2 × 1000lbs bombs or 6 × 5in rockets

DOUGLAS SBD–5 'DAUNTLESS'

Type:	2 seat dive bomber
Date of entering service:	1941 (carried by *Intrepid* 1943–44)
Wingspan:	41ft 6³⁄₈in
Wing area:	326sq ft
Length:	32ft 6in
Weight:	6675lbs (net), 9530lbs (normal load)
Speed:	229mph at sea level, 253mph at 16,600ft
Engine:	1200hp, 9cyl, Wright R1820–60
Fuel capacity:	260gal (plus 2×58 gal drop tanks)
Range:	1300 miles at 144mph
Ceiling:	26,500ft
Armament:	2–0.50cal MG (360rpg), 2–0.30cal MG (2000rpg); 1 × 1600lbs, 1000lbs or 500lbs bomb/or 2 × 325lbs bombs or 1 to 3 depth charges

GRUMMAN TBF–1/TBM–1 and –3 'AVENGER'

Type:	3 seat torpedo bomber
Date of entering service:	1942 (TBM–3 1944) (carried by *Intrepid* throughout war service)
Wingspan:	54ft 2in
Wing area:	490 sq ft
Length:	40ft
Weight:	10,600lbs (net), 16,300lbs (loaded); TBM–3 – 10,700/16,400lbs
Speed:	247mph at sea level, 259mph at 11,200ft; TBM–3 – 262mph at 16,600ft
Engine:	1850hp Wright R2600-8; TBM–3 – 1900hp Wright R2600 – 20
Fuel capacity:	335 gal (plus 2–100gal drop tanks)
Range:	1020 (TBM–3 – 1000) miles (loaded) at 125mph
Ceiling:	23,000ft (TBM–3 – 25,000ft)
Armament:	3 – 0.05cal MG, 1 – 0.30cal MG, 8 – 60lbs rockets, 1 × 22in torpedo or 1 × 2000 or 1600lbs bomb or 2 × 1000lbs bombs or 4 × 500lbs bombs or 12 – 100lbs bombs
Note:	Early model TBF–1/TBM–1 (TBF built by Grumman, TBM by General Motors) superseded by TBM–3 in later years of war

CHANCE VOUGHT F4U–1/F4U–4 'CORSAIR'

Type:	Single seat fighter bomber
Date of entering service:	1942 (carried by *Intrepid* 1944-45)
Wingspan:	40ft 11in; F4U-4 – 39ft 8in
Wing area:	314sq ft; F4U-4 – 305sq ft
Length:	33ft 4in; F4U-4 – 33ft 8in
Weight:	8694lbs (net), 12,039lbs (normal load); F4U-4 – 9205/12,420lbs
Speed:	328mph at sea level, 425mph at 20,000ft; F4U-4 381mph at sea level, 446mph at 26,200ft
Engine:	2250hp, 18cyl Pratt and Witney R2800 – 8W; F4U-4 – 2450hp, R2800 – 18W
Range:	1015 miles (normal) at 185mph
Ceiling:	37,000ft; F4U-4 – 41,500ft
Armament:	6 × 0.5cal MG (400rpg), 2 × 1000lbs bombs or 8 × 5in rockets

CURTISS SB2C 'HELLDIVER'

Type:	2 seat drive bomber
Date of entering service:	1942 (carried by *Intrepid* 1944-45)
Wingspan:	49ft 8⁵⁄₈in
Wing area:	422sq ft
Length:	36ft 9in
Weight:	10,114lbs (net), 13,674lbs (normal load)
Speed:	265mph at sea level, 281mph at 12,400ft
Engine:	1700hp, 14cyl Wright R2600-8
Fuel capacity:	320 gal
Range:	110 miles at 158mph
Ceiling:	24,200ft
Armament:	2-20mm MG (400rpg), 2-0.3cal MG (1000rpg), 1 × 2000lbs or 1600lbs bombs, or 2 × 1000lbs or 500lbs bombs or one torpedo or 1 to 2 depth charges (plus 2 × 100lbs bombs or 2 depth charges under wing)

TABLE 4: **PARTICULARS OF GUNS**

5in/38 Mk 12

Calibre:	5in
Length of bore:	38cal (190in)
Length of gun:	15ft 10in (oa)
Weight of gun:	1 ton 15cwt 70lbs (including BM)
Weight of shell:	54lbs (High Capacity), 55lbs (AA common)
Weight of burster:	7.55lbs
Weight of charge:	15,5lbs
Chamber pressure:	18 tons per sq in
Muzzle velocity:	2600fps
Muzzle energy:	2580ft-tons
Maximum range:	18,200yds at 45°; 37,200ft at 85°
Rifling:	Uniform RH twist, 1 turn in 30 calibres, 157.2in long
Mounting:	Twin Mk 32 and single Mk 30
Maximum elevation:	85°
Maximum depression:	15°
Weight of mounting:	53 tons 14 cwt (twin including guns)
Maximum rate of fire:	15rpm

40mm Bofors Mk 1 and 2

Calibre:	40mm (1.575in)
Length of bore:	60cal (96in)
Length of gun:	130in
Weight of gun:	5cwt 56lbs
Weight of shell:	2lbs
Weight of burster:	1.15lbs
Weight of charge:	0.694lbs
Chamber pressure:	19.5tons per sq in
Muzzle velocity:	2890fps
Maximum range:	11,000yds at 42°; 22,800ft at 90° (max effective range 2500yds)
Rifling:	16 grooves, RH twist × 75.85in long
Mounting:	Quadruple Mk 2
Maximum elevation:	90°
Maximum depression:	15°
Weight of mounting:	10.5 tons (including guns)
Rate of fire:	120rpm
Gun crew:	11 per quadruple mounting

20mm Oerlikon

Calibre:	20mm (0.787in)
Length of bore:	70cal
Length of gun:	87in
Weight of gun:	1cwt 29lbs (including BM)
Weight of shell:	0.27lbs
Weight of charge:	27.7 grams
Muzzle velocity:	2740fps
Maximum range:	6250yds at 45°; 10,000ft at 87° (max effective range 1000yds)
Rifling:	9 grooves, RH twist, 1 turn in 36 calibres
Mounting:	Single Mk 4 and twin Mk 24
Maximum elevation:	87°
Maximum depression:	5°
Weight of mounting:	1695lbs (single, including gun)
Maximum rate of fire:	450rpm

TABLE 5: PARTICULARS OF RADAR

SK-1

Type:	Long range air search
Wavelength:	1.5m
Frequency:	195MHz ('P' band)
Peak power:	200kW
Pulse:	60 pulses/sec of 5 microseconds
Range:	100nm on target at 10,000ft (minimum range 1200yds)
Beam width:	20° horizontal and vertical
Accuracy:	Range–plus and minus 150yds (short range scale); bearing – plus and minus 3°; altitude – plus and minus 2000ft
Antenna:	17ft × 17ft reflector, 36 dipoles (6×6), weight 4900lbs, power rotation 0 to 4.5rpm
Display:	12in PPI with 20, 75 and 200 mile scales. 5in 'A' scan with 15, 75 and 375 mile scales
Associate IFF:	BL-5 (antenna fitted on top of SK antenna)

SC-2

Note:	This was the same set as SK but employed a different antenna; particulars are as given for SK except for following:
Range:	80nm on target at 10,000ft
Beam width:	20° horizontal, 60° vertical
Antenna:	15ft × 4ft 6in reflector, 12 dipoles (6×2)

SM

Type:	Low angle air search/height finding (fighter control)
Wavelength:	10cm
Frequency:	2800MHz ('S' Band)
Peak Power:	600–700kW
Pulse:	775–825 pulses/sec of 1 microsecond
Range:	50nm on target at 10,000ft (25–30nm on surface target), minimum 600yds
Beam width:	2.5° horizontal, 3° vertical; 4° horizontal, 4.5° vertical (with conical scan)
Accuracy:	Range – plus and minus 200yds (or ¼ per cent of range scale whichever is greater); bearing and altitude – plus and minus ⅓° (with conical scan)
Antenna:	Stabilised 96in parabolic dish reflector, with spinning waveguide for 5° conical scan; weight 4400lbs; elevation range 75° to −3°; power rotation at 2 or 6rpm
Display:	PPI (10, 50 and 80 mile scales)
Associate IFF:	BM (antenna fitted on SM antenna)

SG-1

Type:	Surface search
Wavelength:	10cm
Frequency:	3000MHz ('S' band)
Peak Power:	50Kw
Pulse:	c800 pulses/sec of 2 microseconds
Range:	15–22 miles (minimum 600yds)
Beamwidth:	5.6° horizontal, 15° vertical
Accuracy:	Range – plus and minus 200yds (on 15,000yd range scale); bearing – plus and minus 2°
Antenna:	Cut parabola, 48in × 15in; power rotation at 4, 8 or 12rpm; weight 340lbs
Display:	5in 'A' scan and 9in PPI (15,000yd and 75,000yd range scales)
Associate IFF:	BK (separate ski-pole antenna)

Mk 4

Type:	AA fire control for Mk 37 director
Wavelength:	40cm
Frequency:	'L' Band
Pulse:	1.5 microseconds
Range:	Aircraft 40,000yds, surface vessels 10,000–20,000yds, minimum 1000yds
Beamwidth:	9° horizontal and vertical (15° with lobing on)
Accuracy:	Range – plus and minus 50yds; bearing – plus and minus 4 mils; elevation – plus and minus 5 mils above 10°
Antenna:	Stabilised, 6ft × 6ft double reflector, 8 dipoles (2×4)
Display:	'A' scope (100,000yd scale)

Mk 12

Type:	AA fire control for Mk 37 director
Wavelength:	33cm
Frequency:	'L' band
Peak power:	100–110kW
Pulse:	480 pulses/sec of 1.2 microseconds
Range:	45,000yds on aircraft, 40,000yds on surface vessels, minimum 400yds
Beamwidth:	7°–10° horizontal, 8°–11° vertical (12°–15° horizontal, 13°–16° vertical with lobing)
Accuracy:	Range – plus and minus 15yds; bearing and elevation – plus and minus 3 mils (slow targets)
Antenna:	as Mk 4
Display:	'A' scope (range scale 50,000yds)

Mk 22

Type:	Low angle height finding in conjunction with Mk 12
Frequency:	'X' band
Peak power:	25–35kW
Pulse:	480 pulses/sec of 0.5 microseconds
Beamwidth:	4.5° horizontal, 1.2° vertical
Accuracy:	Elevation – plus and minus 3 mils
Antenna:	Parabolic 72in × 18in 'Orange peel' reflector, scanning vertically from −7° to +6° on line of sight at 1 cycle per second

The Photographs

1. Port quarter view of *Intrepid* at Norfolk Navy Yard on 11 September 1943 showing her appearance as commissioned.

USN, by courtesy of A D Baker III

2

3

2. Taken from almost directly overhead, the *Intrepid* as built (Norfolk Navy Yard, 11 September 1943). Note that the forward 20mm gun platform on the side of the bridge carries only three mountings. The five small vehicles at the forward end of the flight deck are aircraft towing tractors, which greatly improve the efficiency of aircraft handling on the flight deck and in the hangar. The larger object to port of the tractors is the ship's mobile crane, used for clearing wrecked aircraft as well as more mundane duties. Marked on the flight deck is an outline of the ship's waterline – the purpose of which is a mystery.

USN, by courtesy of A D Baker III

3. *Intrepid*, possibly running trials, in November 1943, showing her early modifications – the rearranged radar rig to accommodate an SM antenna on the masthead platform and the extension of the forward 20mm gun platform on the side of the bridge to accommodate two additional mountings. Note the starboard extension to the hangar deck catapult, hinged up into its stowed position, and the hull number painted in black on the flight deck.

USN, by courtesy of A D Baker III

4. This close-up of *Intrepid*'s bridge on 1 September 1943 shows the ship's original radar rig with the big SK antenna on the masthead platform and the second SG antenna on the pole mast to port of the stack. The SC antenna, on the starboard side of the stack, is largely hidden by the mast while the pole mast at the rear of the stack is hidden by the SG pole mast. The large box abaft the topmast is a loudspeaker (usually called reproducers in the US Navy) and the two small rectangular boxes on each side of that (mounted on spurs angled up from platform) are the upper flighting lights.

USN, by courtesy of A D Baker III

4

5. In drydock at Pearl Harbor on 26 February 1944, *Intrepid*'s stern showing the hole in the starboard side of the rudder caused by the torpedo hit of 18 February. Note the four, four-bladed screws and the laps in the shell plating.

USN

6. Damage to the starboard side of the 3rd deck aft caused by the torpedo hit of 18 February 1944. This view was taken looking aft from the CPOs' mess (stations 184 – 192½) into the berthing space (stations 192½ – 198), from which all the furniture and most of the separating transverse bulkhead at station 192½ have been removed. Note the deck, and the deck head connections for the removed bulkhead, the two main transverse girders under the second deck (stations 191 and 194) and the shallower but more numerous longitudinal girders. The ship's starboard side is just out of view to the left and the main starboard longitudinal bulkhead can be seen on the right. The box structure at the extreme top of the photograph is a ventilation trunk.

USN

7. The *Intrepid*'s stern taken on 26 May, toward the end of her March – June 1944 refit at Hunters Point, San Francisco. From forward to aft along the edge of the main deck can be seen the starboard quarter 40mm mounting, its Mk 51 director, the screen outboard of the only two 20mm mountings fitted on this deck and, over the fantail, the aftermost 40mm mounting and its Mk 51 director. The after wireless mast is partially lowered – note that the walkway platform on which it stands and the antenna wire screen, (on each side of the mast) also hinge down with the mast. On the platform below the mast are six smoke screen tanks, the vertical chute forward of them being their slide. Note also the three life net racks on the gallery walkways and the two life rafts stowed beneath them. Behind the centre life net rack is one of the flight deck gasoline stations.

USN, by courtesy of A D Baker III

5

6

1259-44-S8   CV11
VIEW AFT SHOWING ALTERATIONS
HUNTERS POINT   26 MAY 1944

8. The *Intrepid*'s starboard quarter on 26 May 1944. The opening in the hangar side below the after twin 5in mounting is one of the boiler room air intakes and the slightly lower opening further aft is a ventilator trunk inlet. The side ladder is raised but not stowed which involved hinging it flat against the ship's side. Under the boat and aircraft crane is one of her two 26ft whaleboats, all that were retained from an intended outfit which included 50ft and 40ft motor launches (which would have been stowed fore and aft of the crane) and a 35ft motor boat (which would have been stowed in the position occupied by the forward 40mm mounting). They were almost certainly omitted (before any of the *Essex* class completed) to save space and topweight and it is possible that if this had been done at the design stage the hangar might have been enlarged by extending it out to the starboard quarter deck edge.

USN, by courtesy of A D Baker II

9. The midships structure on 26 May 1944 with the modifications carried out during her March – June refit circled. From top to bottom these are: YE antenna moved forward of topmast; pole mast on stack provided with new platform for YJ (visible) and SG (yet to be fitted) antennas; masthead platform extended to rear to accommodate SK antenna; new tower on starboard side of funnel for SC antenna; platform forward of pilot house fitted with windscreen, flag bridge platform extended forward and 40mm mounting removed; three Mk 51 directors fitted at ends of 20mm gun platform and three 40mm mountings fitted on hangar side.

USN, by courtesy of A D Baker III

10. A bow view of *Intrepid* at Hunters Point on 26 May 1944 showing the supporting structure under the forward end of the flight deck. The athwartships walkway at the forward end provided access to the underside of the six ramp lights for care and maintenance.

USN, by courtesy of A D Baker III

11. A view looking forward over *Intrepid*'s flight deck taken from the stack top on 26 May 1944. On the right is the back of her forward Mk 37 director and in the foreground, hidden by a canvas cover, her port 24in searchlight. Attached to the screen around the searchlight is one of her whip antennas while forward of the searchlight, in the air defence position, can be seen a sky lookout (with binoculars removed) and target designator. Below on the flight deck adjacent to the island is the top of one of her bomb elevators while further forward the foremost bomb elevator is open. The circle indicates the addition of a second flight deck catapult. Note that although the bow-landing arrester wires have been removed the three barriers, seen here stowed flat on the deck, are still in position – presumably retained to serve as a back-up to those aft.

USN, by courtesy of A D Baker III

12. Looking aft from the IFF antenna platform on the port side of the stack, 26 March 1944. In the immediate left foreground is the horn of the port steam whistle with, above it, a short whip antenna attached via a bracket to the side of the whistle, and beyond the rear of the Mk 4 radar antenna on the after Mk 37 director. The circles indicate the additional port side 40mm mountings and the fact that the 20mm gun platforms have been moved forward to clear positions for them.

USN, by courtesy of A D Baker III

13. *Intrepid* sails from Hunters Point on 9 June 1944, her flight deck loaded with aircraft and vehicles for the Pacific War – it was common practice to use carriers returning to the war zone as transports in this way.

USN, by courtesy of A D Baker III

14. The complementary starboard side version of the previous photograph, 9 June 1944.

USN, by courtesy of A D Baker III

11

12

13

14

15. A Hellcat takes off from the *Ticonderoga* (CV14) in October 1944. The bridge structure and detail is generally similar to *Intrepid*'s after her 1944 refit, except principally for the arrangement of windshields at the fore end of the platforms, the placing of the main signal yard forward instead of abaft the tripod mast, the lack of a pole mast on the stack, the Mk 12/22 radar on the Mk 37 directors (not fitted in *Intrepid* until 1945) and several variations in the arrangement of radio and ECM antennas.

USN

16. Looking forward from the *Intrepid*'s port 36in searchlight platform on 25 October 1944. In the foreground is the primary fly control station from which flight deck operations were monitored. The row of boxes along the inside of the control station's screen are the switches for the various flight deck lighting circuits (landing lights, ramp lights, etc). The screen and the bulkhead behind it also carried equipment, and the associate junction boxes and switches, for communication with aircraft and flight deck personnel via telephone, loudspeaker or radio. The canvas cover on the right is over the ladderway to the platform below and the box on the side of the 24in searchlight platform at the top of the picture is the base of one of the whip antennas.

USN

17. After her early 1945 refit *Intrepid* sails from Hunters Point, again loaded with aircraft for temporary service as a transport, en route for the war zone (20 February 1945). The circled alterations carried out during this refit are from forward: replacement of Mk 4 by Mk 12/22 radar on the Mk 37 directors; shortened lattice tower for the SG radar antenna on the stack, new starboard quarter 40mm sponson; and new fantail sponson for two 40mm mountings. She is in her final wartime paint scheme – Measure 12 – sea blue below the main deck and ocean grey above.

USN, by courtesy of A D Baker III

16

17

18. Viewed from the main deck, the hole in *Intrepid*'s flight deck caused by the Kamikaze hit of 16 April 1945. The corrugated sheets of metal hanging from the deck head are the remains of walkways, undamaged examples of which are just visible at bottom left beyond the deep transverse girder or 'bent'. The longitudinal flight deck girders, with lightening holes, are laid across the top of the transverse bents, the latter constructed of plates stiffened with riders at top and bottom and a framework of 'T' bars on the face.

USN

19. *Intrepid* from directly astern on 20 February 1945 with her newly fitted 40mm gun sponsons circled. At the outer edges of the centre circle the two aftermost flight deck foundations can be seen angling up to support the aftermost bent.

USN, by courtesy of A D Baker III

18

19

The Drawings

A NOTE ON THE DRAWINGS

The drawings are all based on official US Navy plans for the construction of the *Essex* class. The general arrangements in this book are generally reproduced at 1/300 (25ft = 1in) or 1/600 (50ft = 1in) scales, with the details produced whenever possible to simple enlargements or reductions of those scales (*ie* 1/150, 1/75, 1/37.5, etc). Scales are noted in the headings to the keys where applicable.

A General arrangements

A1/1 PORT SIDE FORWARD (A1-A 4 drawings
are 1/300 scale)

A1/2 PORT SIDE AFT

A1/1

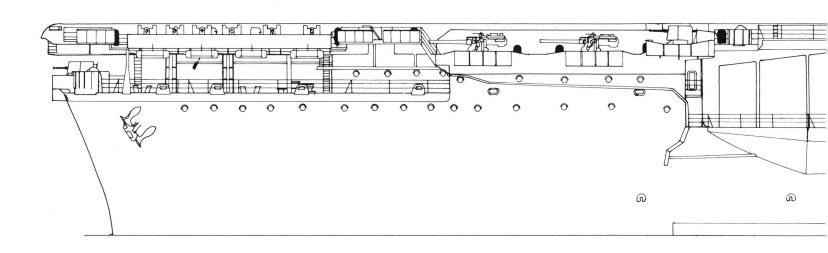

A1/2

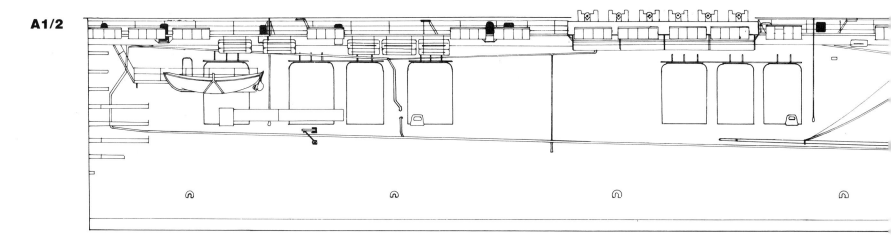

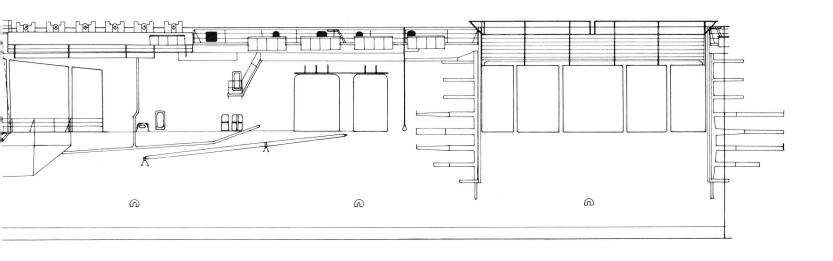

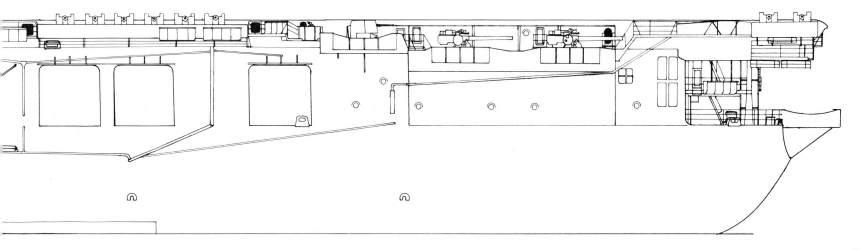

A2/2

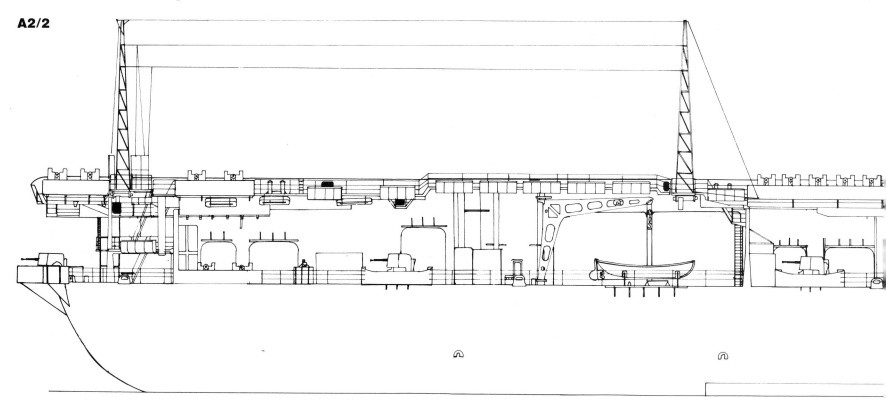

A2/1

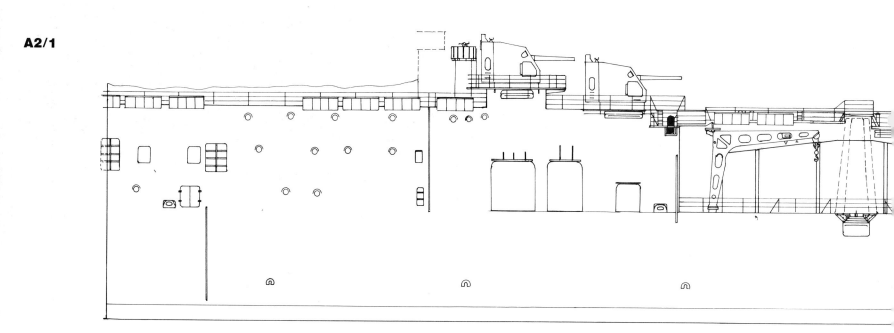

A2/1   STARBOARD SIDE FORWARD

A2/2   STARBOARD SIDE AFT

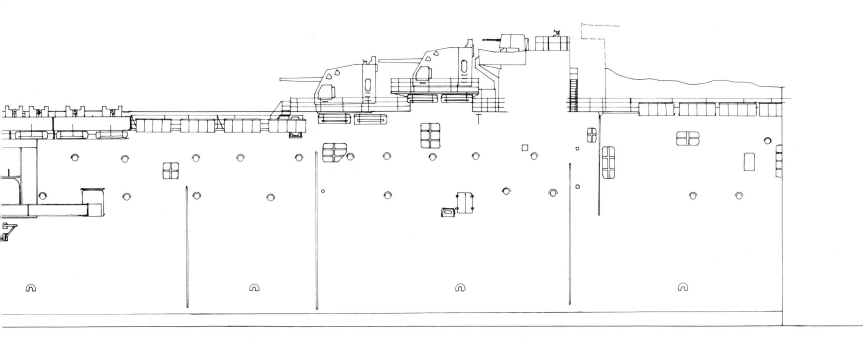

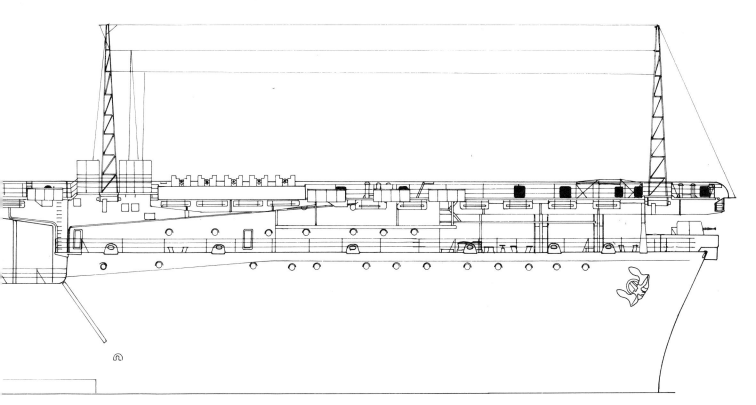

A General arrangements

1	Walkway	16	Panama sight	31	Boiler uptake
2	Outline of gallery walkways, gun sponsons etc	17	Deck drains in waterways around deck edge	32	Passage
		18	Removable cover	33	Crew's WC
3	Platform with ladder to walkway	19	Elevator controls	34	Radio 6
4	Vertical ladder	20	Waterway on deck around elevator opening	35	Ammunition hoist
5	Antenna mast	21	5inch/38 twin DP gun mounting	36	Fire-control tube
6	Arrester wire (chaffing plate under)	22	Aircraft barrier (chaffing plate under)	37	Expansion joint
7	Blue painted stripe	23	Bomb elevator	38	Air hose reel
8	Aircraft securing tracks	24	Bomb elevator controls	39	Sloping bulkhead
9	Landing lights	25	Life nets	40	Repair room
10	Ramp lights	26	5in handling room and ready service ammunition	41	Squadron locker
11	Catapult			42	Pilot balloon room
12	Signal platform (wood grating)	27	Flight deck control	43	Torpedo elevator
13	Hinged canvas screen	28	Flight deck crew	44	Torpedo elevator controls
14	Side (navigation) lights	29	Officers' WC		
15	Steering staff	30	Air intakes		

A4/1

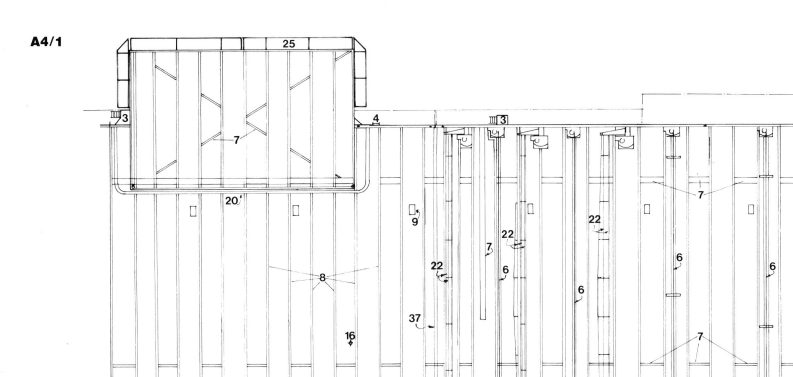

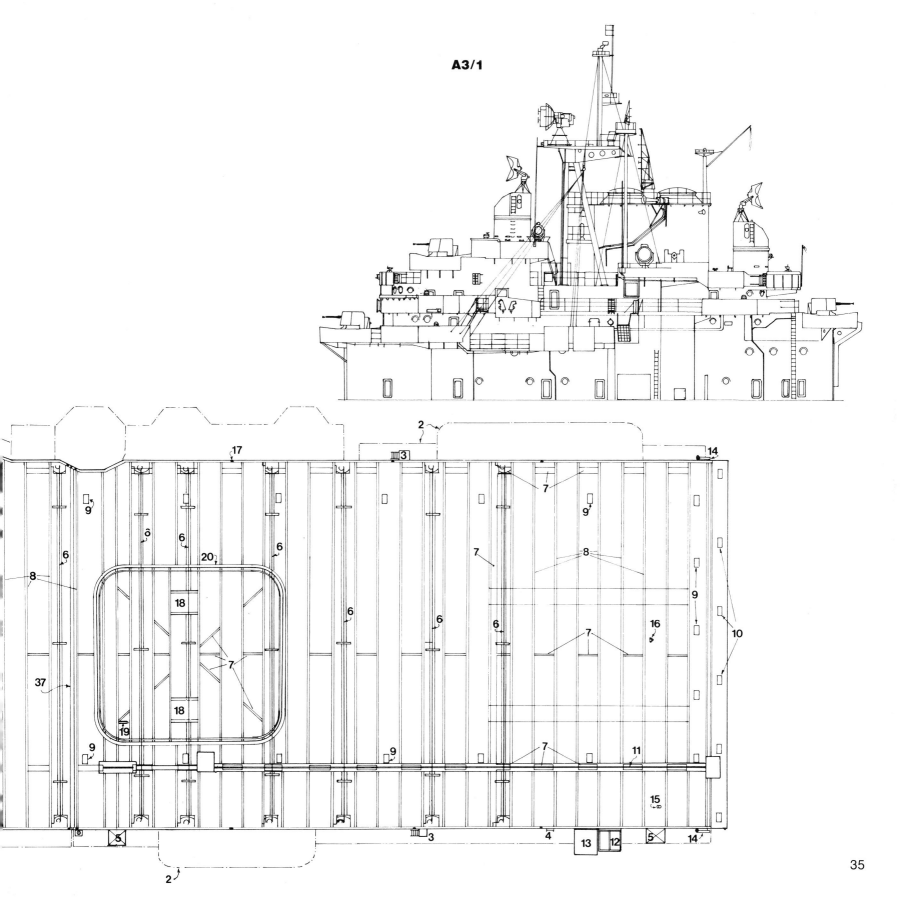

A3/1

35

A General arrangements

A3/2

A4/2

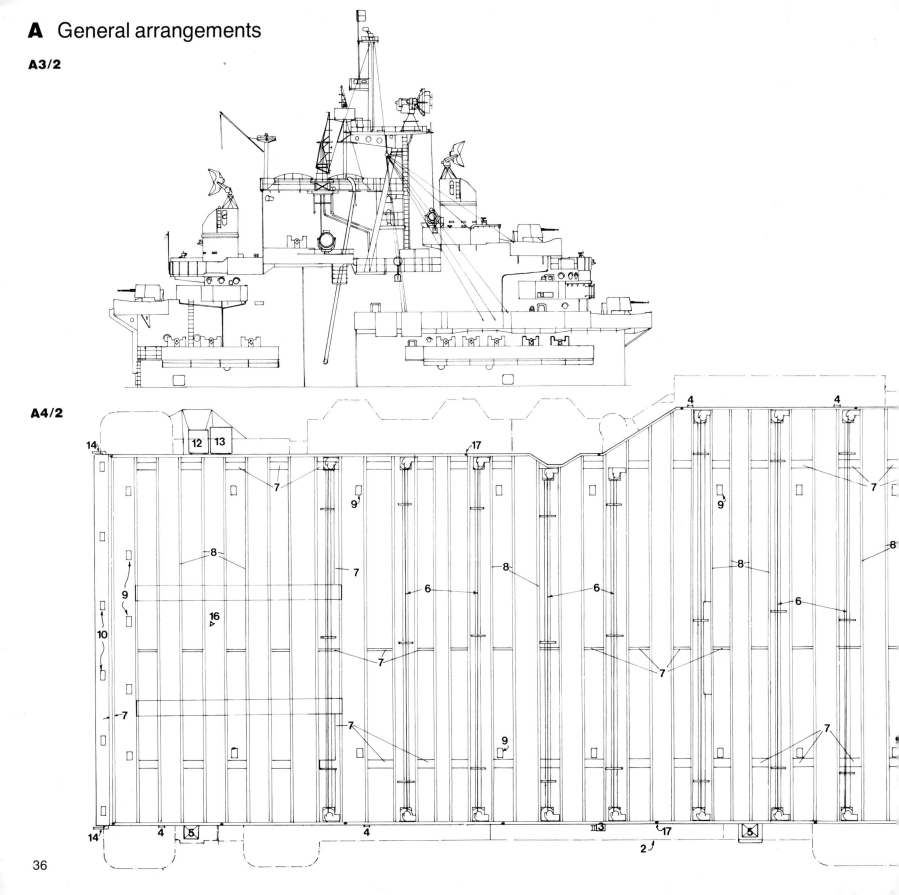

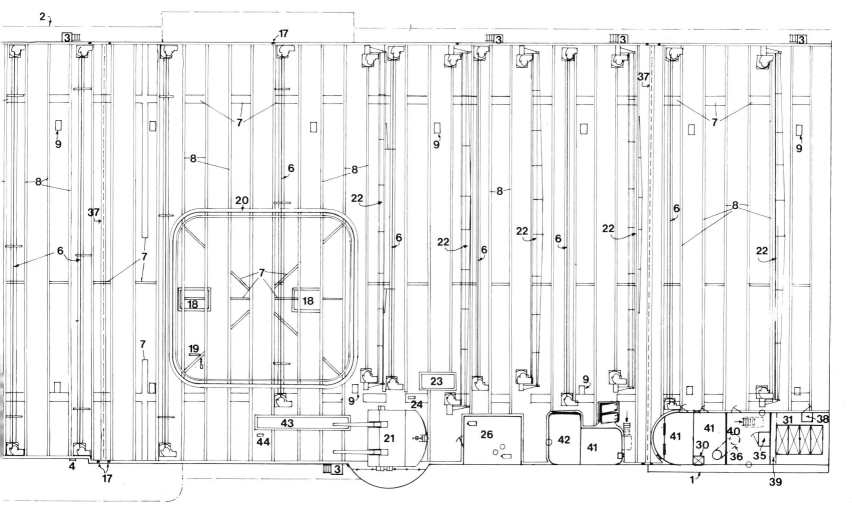

A General arrangements

A5/1 MAST TOP PLATFORMS (all A5 drawings 1/150 scale)

1	SC radar platform
2	Radar platform (not occupied by an antenna)
3	SG radar platform
4	Blinker light
5	Battle gaff
6	BK antenna (IFF)
7	Truck light
8	YE antenna mast
9	Access manhole
10	Outline of stack (under)

A5/1

A5/2

A5/3

A5/4

A5/5

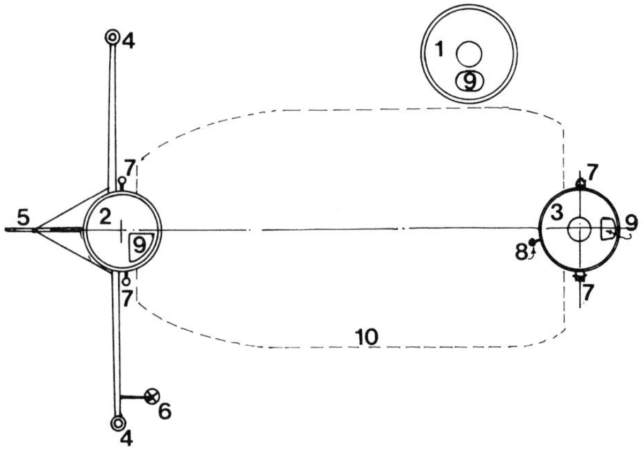

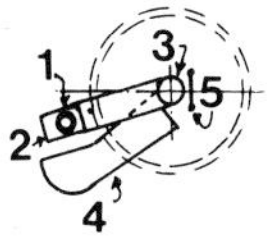

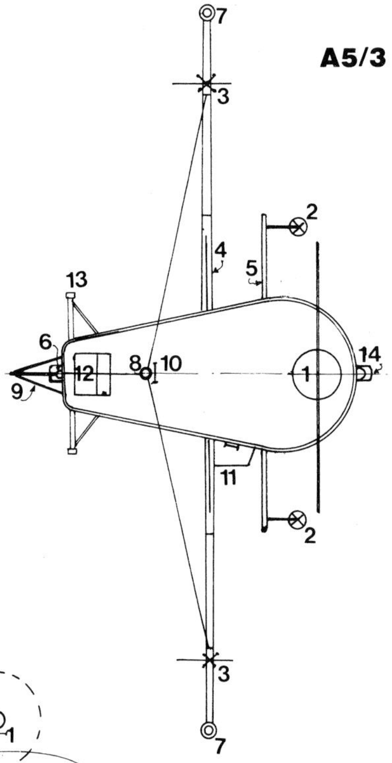

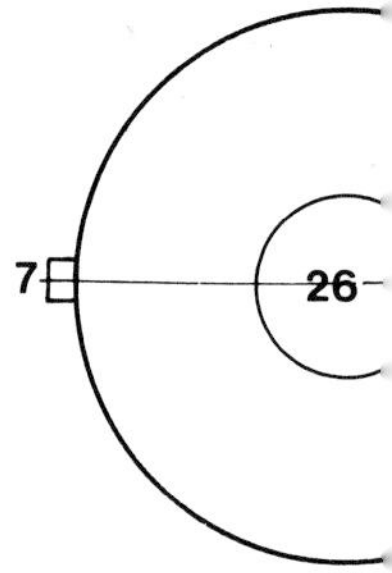

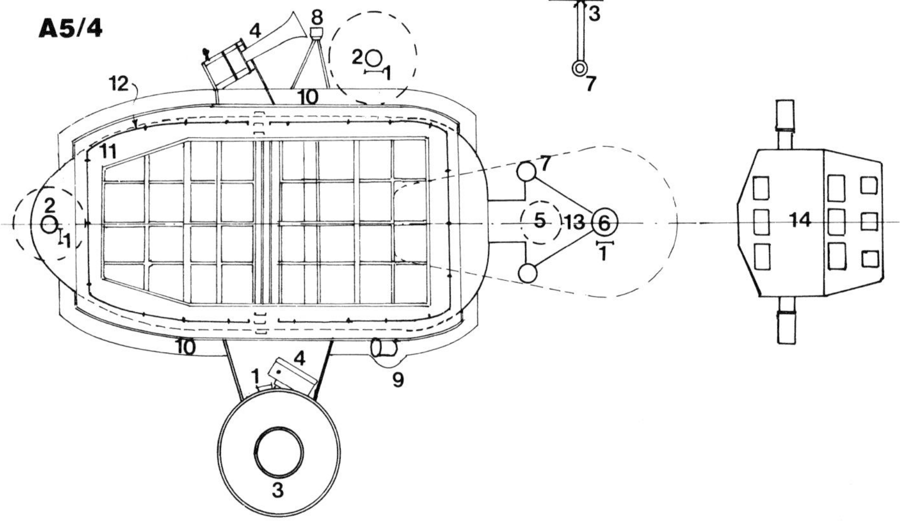

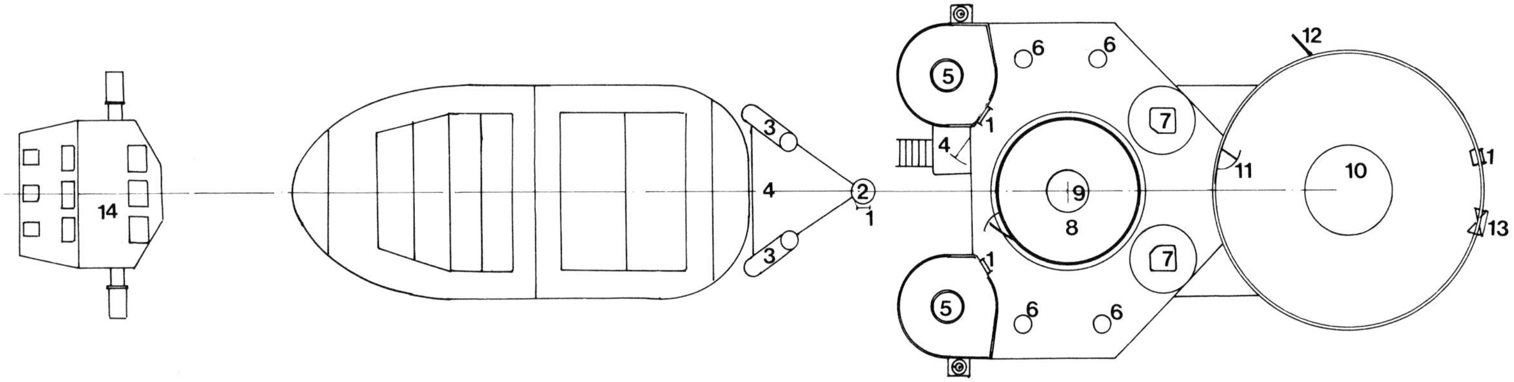

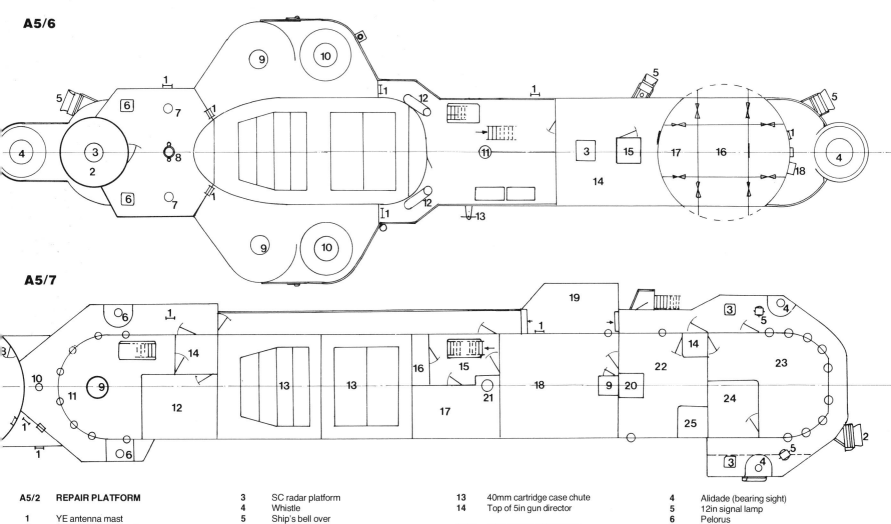

A5/6

A5/7

A5/2	**REPAIR PLATFORM**	**3**	SC radar platform	**13**	40mm cartridge case chute	**4**	Alidade (bearing sight)
		4	Whistle	**14**	Top of 5in gun director	**5**	12in signal lamp
1	YE antenna mast	**5**	Ship's bell over			**6**	Pelorus
2	YE antenna drive unit	**6**	Mast	**A5/6**	**TOP OF PILOT HOUSE**	**7**	40mm cartridge case chute
3	Topmast	**7**	Mast struts			**8**	Ammunition passing scuttle
4	Hinged platform (down)	**8**	Intermediate fighting light (port and	**1**	Vertical ladder	**9**	Fire-control tube
5	Jacobs ladder		starboard)	**2**	Surface lookouts	**10**	Wiring tube
		9	Trash burner smoke pipe	**3**	Fire-control tube	**11**	Secondary conning station
A5/3	**MAST HEAD PLATFORM**	**10**	Grating	**4**	40mm AA director	**12**	Radar control room
		11	Hood	**5**	Loudspeaker	**13**	Boiler uptakes
1	SK radar antenna	**12**	Rail	**6**	Target designator	**14**	Light lock
2	BK antenna	**13**	Platform	**7**	Sky lookout	**15**	Passage
3	Anemometer and wind vane	**14**	Top of 5in gun director	**8**	Compass	**16**	WC
4	Signal yard			**9**	Single 20mm Oerlikon AA guns	**17**	Radar 1
5	Speed flag yard	**A5/5**	**AIR DEFENCE FORWARD AND SKY**	**10**	36in searchlight	**18**	Air plot
6	Range light		**LOOKOUTS**	**11**	Mast	**19**	Primary fly control station
7	Blinker light			**12**	Mast struts	**20**	40mm ammunition hoist
8	Topmast	**1**	Vertical ladder	**13**	Direction finding loop	**21**	Mast
9	Topmast backstay spreader	**2**	Mast	**14**	40mm ready service ammunition	**22**	Chart house
10	Jacobs ladder	**3**	Mast struts	**15**	40mm ammunition hoist	**23**	Pilot house
11	Platform (6ft below) with vertical ladder	**4**	Platform	**16**	Wiring trunk	**24**	Captain's sea cabin
12	Loudspeaker	**5**	24in searchlight	**17**	Void	**25**	WC and shower
13	Upper fighting lights	**6**	Sky lookouts	**18**	40mm cartridge case chute	**26**	Quadruple 40mm Bofors mounting
14	Navigation light	**7**	Target designator			**27**	Davit
		8	Surface lookouts	**A5/7**	**NAVIGATING BRIDGE**		
A5/4	**STACK TOP**	**9**	Fire-control tube				
		10	40mm Bofors quadruple AA mounting	**1**	Vertical ladder		
1	Vertical ladder	**11**	Ammunition passing scuttle	**2**	Loudspeaker		
2	Antenna mast	**12**	Davit	**3**	Target designator		

A General arrangements

A5/8

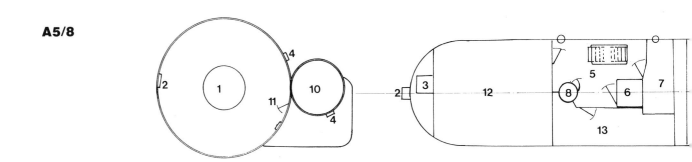

A5/9

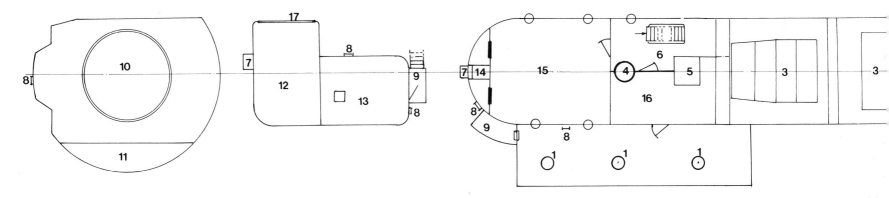

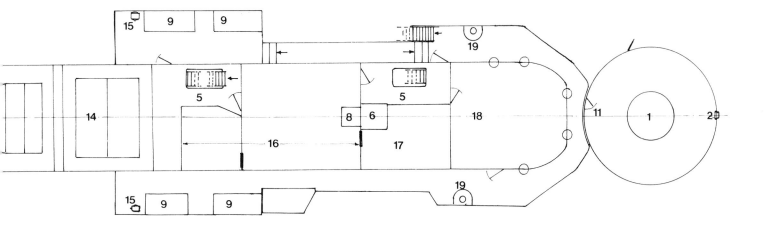

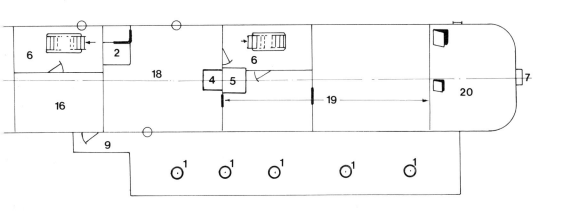

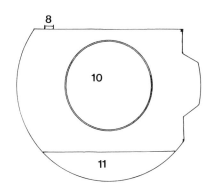

41

A General arrangements

A6/1

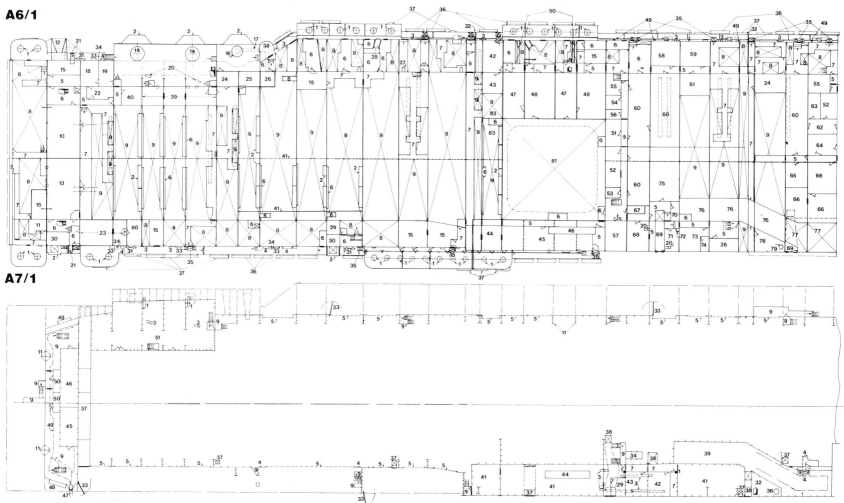

A7/1

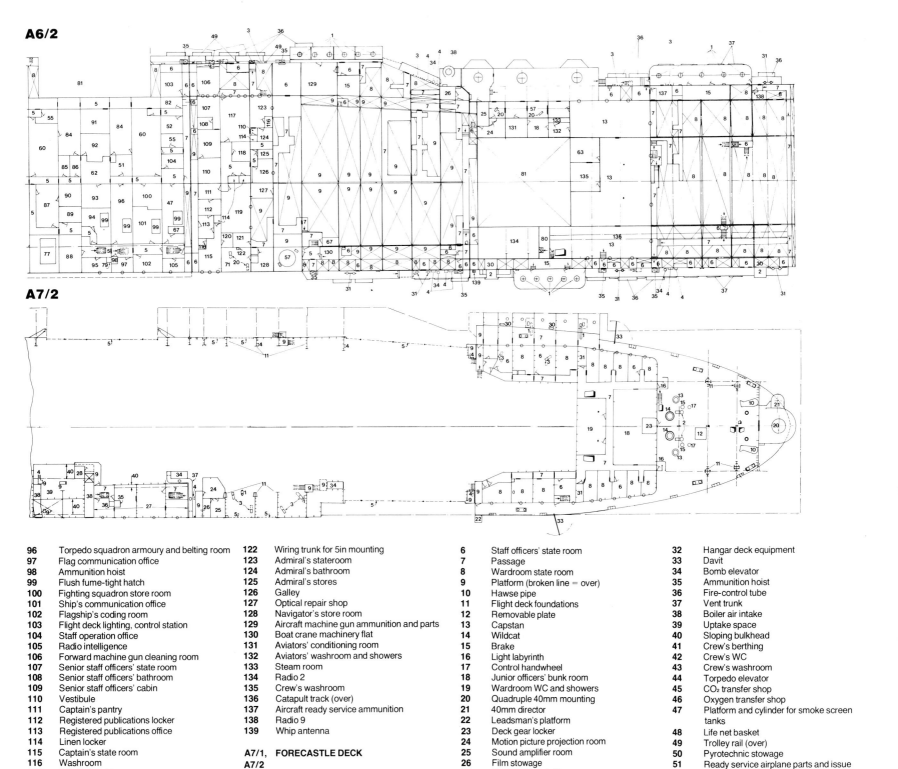

A6/2

A7/2

96 Torpedo squadron armoury and belting room	**122** Wiring trunk for 5in mounting	**6** Staff officers' state room	**32** Hangar deck equipment
97 Flag communication office	**123** Admiral's stateroom	**7** Passage	**33** Davit
98 Ammunition hoist	**124** Admiral's bathroom	**8** Wardroom state room	**34** Bomb elevator
99 Flush fume-tight hatch	**125** Admiral's stores	**9** Platform (broken line = over)	**35** Ammunition hoist
100 Fighting squadron store room	**126** Galley	**10** Hawse pipe	**36** Fire-control tube
101 Ship's communication office	**127** Optical repair shop	**11** Flight deck foundations	**37** Vent trunk
102 Flagship's coding room	**128** Navigator's store room	**12** Removable plate	**38** Boiler air intake
103 Flight deck lighting, control station	**129** Aircraft machine gun ammunition and parts	**13** Capstan	**39** Uptake space
104 Staff operation office	**130** Boat crane machinery flat	**14** Wildcat	**40** Sloping bulkhead
105 Radio intelligence	**131** Aviators' conditioning room	**15** Brake	**41** Crew's berthing
106 Forward machine gun cleaning room	**132** Aviators' washroom and showers	**16** Light labyrinth	**42** Crew's WC
107 Senior staff officers' state room	**133** Steam room	**17** Control handwheel	**43** Crew's washroom
108 Senior staff officers' bathroom	**134** Radio 2	**18** Junior officers' bunk room	**44** Torpedo elevator
109 Senior staff officers' cabin	**135** Crew's washroom	**19** Wardroom WC and showers	**45** CO_2 transfer shop
110 Vestibule	**136** Catapult track (over)	**20** Quadruple 40mm mounting	**46** Oxygen transfer shop
111 Captain's pantry	**137** Aircraft ready service ammunition	**21** 40mm director	**47** Platform and cylinder for smoke screen tanks
112 Registered publications locker	**138** Radio 9	**22** Leadsman's platform	
113 Registered publications office	**139** Whip antenna	**23** Deck gear locker	**48** Life net basket
114 Linen locker		**24** Motion picture projection room	**49** Trolley rail (over)
115 Captain's state room	**A7/1, FORECASTLE DECK**	**25** Sound amplifier room	**50** Pyrotechnic stowage
116 Washroom	**A7/2**	**26** Film stowage	**51** Ready service airplane parts and issue room
117 Admiral's cabin	**1** 5in mounting wiring trunk	**27** Air department office	
118 Admiral's pantry	**2** Chain pipes	**28** Hangar deck conflagration station	
119 Captain's cabin	**3** 5in ammunition hoist	**29** Showers	
120 Captain's bathroom	**4** Vertical ladder	**30** Mooring ring	
121 Gasoline gear locker	**5** Roller curtain	**31** Linen locker	

A General arrangements

A8/1

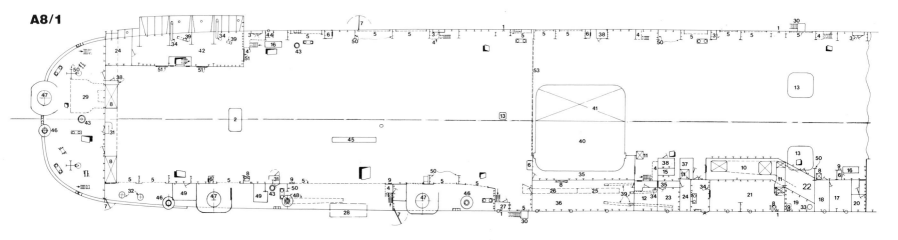

A9/1

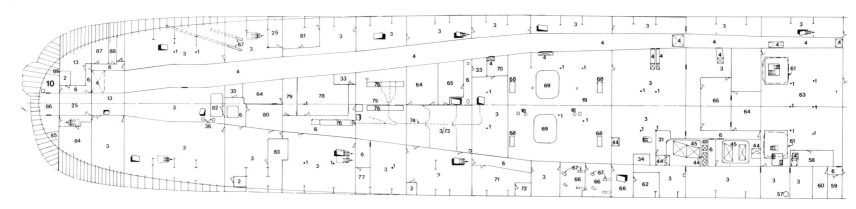

A8/1,	**MAIN (HANGAR) DECK**		**25**	Torpedo elevator (over)	**53**	Canvas curtain
A8/2			**26**	Portable torpedo ramp	**54**	Elevator cable pipe
			27	Deck office	**55**	Office and copy room
1	Expansion joint (in side plating)		**28**	Portable platform for handling planes	**56**	Stock room
2	Aviation engine hatch		**29**	5in twin loading machine (training)	**57**	Finishing room
3	Gasoline filling station		**30**	Accommodation ladder	**58**	Contact printing room
4	Platform (over)		**31**	Light labyrinth	**59**	Enlarging room
5	Roller curtain		**32**	Single 20mm Oerlikon mounting	**60**	Chemical mixing room
6	Hangar sprinkling control station		**33**	Fire-control tube	**61**	Motion picture developing room
7	Davit		**34**	5in gun mounting wiring trunk	**62**	Compressor room
8	Vent trunk		**35**	Passage	**63**	Ready service bomb fuzes
9	Vertical ladder		**36**	Crew's berthing	**64**	Raincoats
10	Boiler uptake		**37**	Repair locker	**65**	Hinged catapult extensions
11	Air intake		**38**	Aircraft ready use ammunition	**66**	Walkways
12	Diving gear		**39**	5in ammunition hoist	**67**	Deck gear locker
13	Removable plate		**40**	Elevator opening	**68**	Gasoline repair station
14	Storage battery shop		**41**	Auxiliary elevator	**69**	Senior aviators' state room
15	Bomb elevator		**42**	Aviation repair shop	**70**	Wardroom state room
16	Auxiliary generator set		**43**	Capstan	**71**	Ramp
17	Trash burner room		**44**	Urinal	**72**	Catapult tracks
18	Trash storage space		**45**	Torpedo hatch	**73**	Gunnery officers' state room
19	Hangar deck equipment		**46**	40mm director	**74**	Communication officers' state room
20	Battery workshop		**47**	Quadruple 40mm mounting	**75**	Chaplain's state room
21	Blacksmith, boiler, shipfitter, pipe,		**48**	Boat and aircraft crane	**76**	Supply officers' state room
	coppersmith sheet metal and plumber shop		**49**	Potato stowage	**77**	Assistant gunnery officers' state room
22	Bomb and torpedo, truck and skid stowage		**50**	Flight deck foundation	**78**	40mm ready service ammunition
23	Aviation electrical shop		**51**	Vertical sliding door	**79**	Boatswain's stores
24	Aviation tool issue room		**52**	Deck edge elevator	**80**	Cleaning gear locker

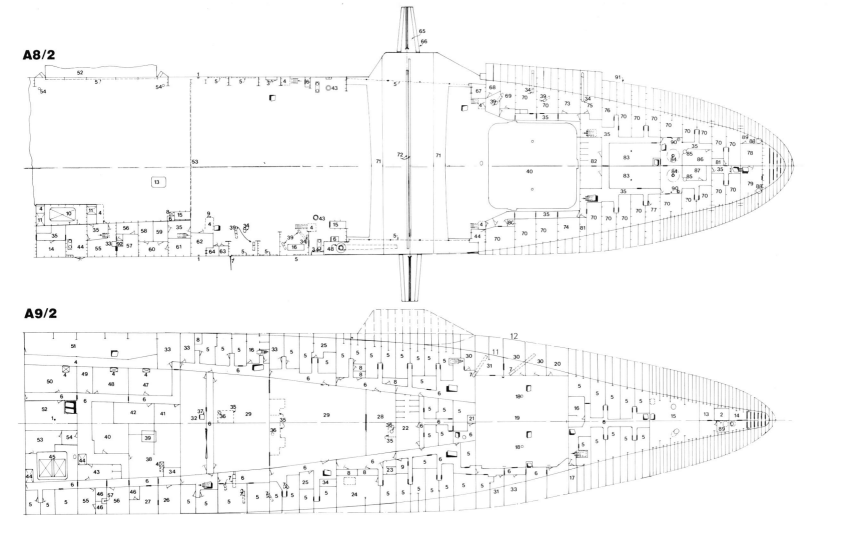

A8/2

A9/2

81	Linen locker	13	SD stores	41	Navigator's office	69	Auxiliary elevator platforms (below main deck)
82	Wardroom WC and showers	14	Boatswain's stores	42	Supply office financial section	70	Peacoat locker
83	Junior officers' bunk room	15	Windlass room	43	Officers' WC and showers	71	Crew's reception room and library
84	Wildcat shaft	16	Wardroom WC	44	Boiler room air intake	72	Chaplain's office
85	Chain pipe	17	Cleaning gear locker	45	Boiler uptake	73	Torpedo assembly space
86	Wardroom washroom	18	Elevator cylinders	46	Bathroom	74	Overhead torpedo rails
87	Ward room barber's shop	19	Elevator pit	47	1st Lieutenant and damage control office	75	Torpedo workshop
88	Hawse pipes	20	Paravane gear and deck gear locker	48	Gunnery office	76	Torpedo hatch
89	Gun control electrical equipment room	21	Gas trunk	49	Captain's office	77	Chief bosun mates' state room
90	Capstan shaft	22	Wardroom WC and showers	50	Exeuctive officer's office	78	Carpenter's shop
91	Line of forecastle deck over	23	Guest WC	51	Elevator machinery space	79	Crew's shower
92	Ammunition hoist	24	Boat and airplane crane winch room	52	Engineer officer's office	80	Crew's washroom
		25	Capstan machinery room	53	Trash burner room	81	Crew's washroom and WC
A9/1,	**2nd DECK**	26	Executive officer's cabin	54	Air lock	82	Aviation engine hatch
A9/2		27	Executive officer's state room	55	1st Lieutenant's state room	83	Boat crane and capstan machinery room
		28	Wardroom lounge	56	Air officers' state room	84	Ordnance stores
1	Pillar	29	Wardroom mess room	57	Fire-control tube	85	Void
2	40mm radar room	30	Trunk room	58	Blue uniform and overcoat locker	86	40mm ready service ammunition
3	Crew's berthing	31	Fan room	59	First sergeant of marines' office	87	Dope stowage
4	Vent trunk	32	Wardroom pantry	60	Marines' stores	88	Acid locker
5	Wardroom state room	33	Blower room	61	Removable plate (and over)	89	Water-tight trunk
6	Passage	34	Bomb elevator	62	Garbage disposal		
7	5in ammunition hoist	35	Trunk (under)	63	Marines' berthing		
8	Locker	36	Gas pipe	64	Crew's WC		
9	Linen locker	37	Dumb waiter	65	Crew's washroom and showers		
10	40mm radar and gun control room	38	Flag office	66	5in ammunition handling room		
11	Edge of 2nd deck	39	Removable plate (over)	67	5in ammunition hoists		
12	Edge of main deck (over)	40	Supply office stores section	68	Main elevator guide and guide pit		

A General arrangements

A10/1

A11/1

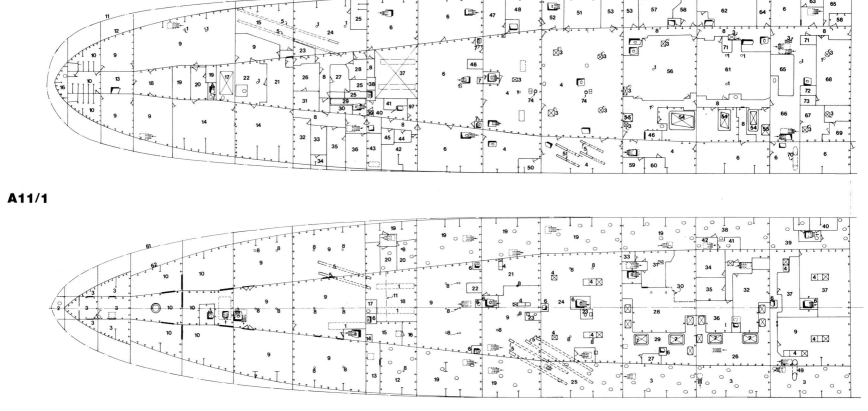

A 10/2

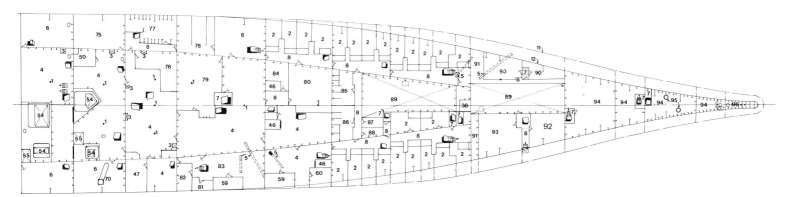

A11/2

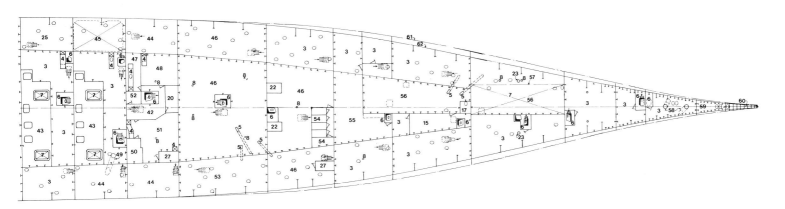

A General arrangements

A12/2

A13/2

A14/2

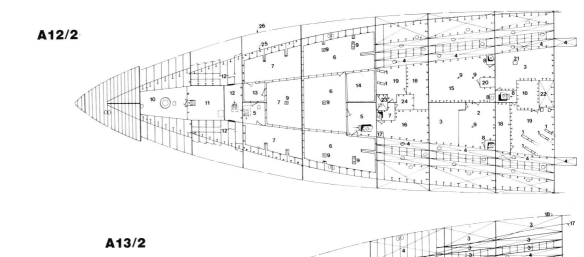

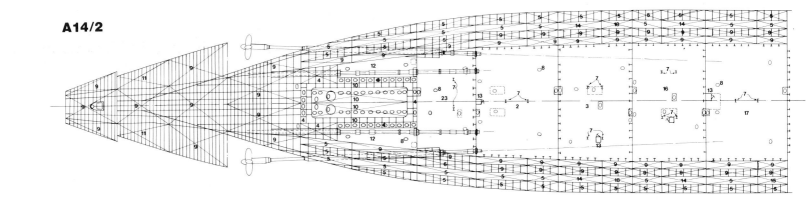

13	Refrigeration machinery room	8	Manholes	25	Aviation lubricating oil pump room
14	Alcohol store	9	Void	26	Aviation lubricating oil
15	Sensitised film store	10	Gasoline tank	27	40mm AA ammunition
16	Line of knuckle in deck (port and starboard)	11	Aviation stores	28	Rocket bombs
17	Line of second platform at side	12	Shaft alley	29	20mm and 0.5cal aircraft ammunition
18	Line of first platform (over)	13	Escape and access trunks	30	CIC (Combat Information Centre)
19	Alcohol locker	14	Service fuel oil	31	Forward auxiliary machinery room
		15	Contaminated oil	32	No 1 boiler room
A14/1, HOLD		16	No 3 boiler room	33	No 2 boiler room
A14/2		17	No 1 machinery room	34	Stores
		18	Fuel oil overflow	35	Pump room
1	Hatch (over)	19	Peak tanks		
2	No 2 machinery room	20	Incendiary bombs		
3	No 4 boiler room	21	Pyrotechnic stowage		
4	Cofferdam	22	Elevator machinery and pump room		
5	Fuel oil or ballast	23	Aft auxiliary machinery room		
6	Diesel oil	24	Fuel oil transfer pump room		
7	Pillar				

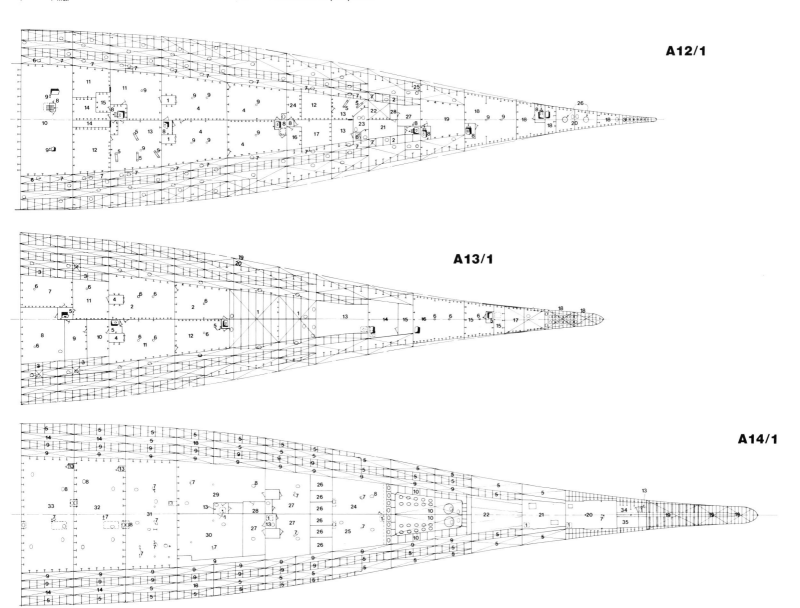

A12/1

A13/1

A14/1

A General arrangements

A15/1 **3rd BOTTOM**
A15/2
1   Hatch (over)
2   Gasoline tank
3   Cofferdam
4   Void
5   Manholes
6   Pyrotechnic stowage
7   Fuel oil

A16/1 **DOUBLE BOTTOM**
A16/2
1   Cofferdam (and shaft passage aft)
2   Sump tank (over)
3   Gasoline tanks
4   Fuel oil
5   Void
6   Diesel oil

7   Reserve feed water
8   Fresh water
9   Peak tank

A17/1, **LONGITUDINAL SECTION ON**
A17/2 **CENTRELINE**

a   Flight deck
b   Gallery deck
c   Forecastle deck
d   Main deck
e   2nd deck
f   3rd deck
g   4th deck
h   1st platform
i   2nd platform
j   Hold

1   Store
2   Peak tank
3   Wardroom barbers' shop
4   Walkway
5   Crew's berthing
6   Passage
7   Water-tight trunk
8   Crew's mess
9   Bomb stowage
10   Crew's washroom
11   Elevator platform
12   Optical repair shop
13   Captain's cabin
14   Girder
15   Hangar
16   Elevator pit
17   Wardroom WC
18   Gas trunk

19   Elevator pit
20   Captain's pantry
21   Squadron armoury and belting room
22   Fighting squadron store room
23   Torpedo squadron armoury and belting room
24   Radar repair and maintenance shop
25   Radar spare parts
26   Ship's ACI store
27   Deck gear locker
28   Junior officers' bunk room
29   Wardroom WC and showers
30   Boatswain's stores
31   Chain pipes
32   Windlass room
33   Wardroom state room
34   Wardroom WC and showers
35   Wardroom lounge

A15/2

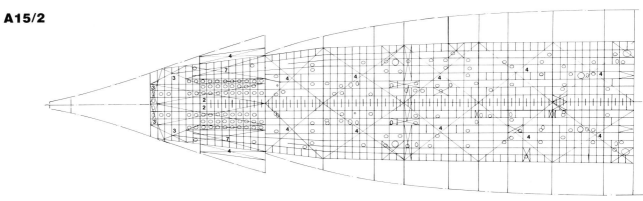

A16/2

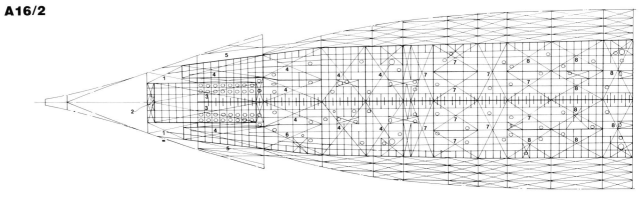

A17/2

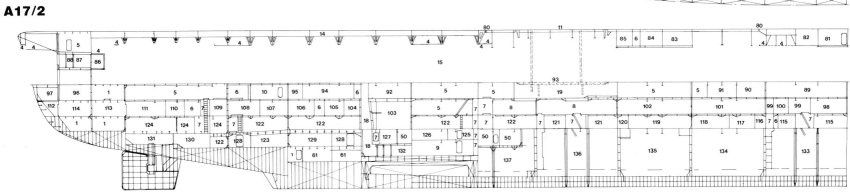

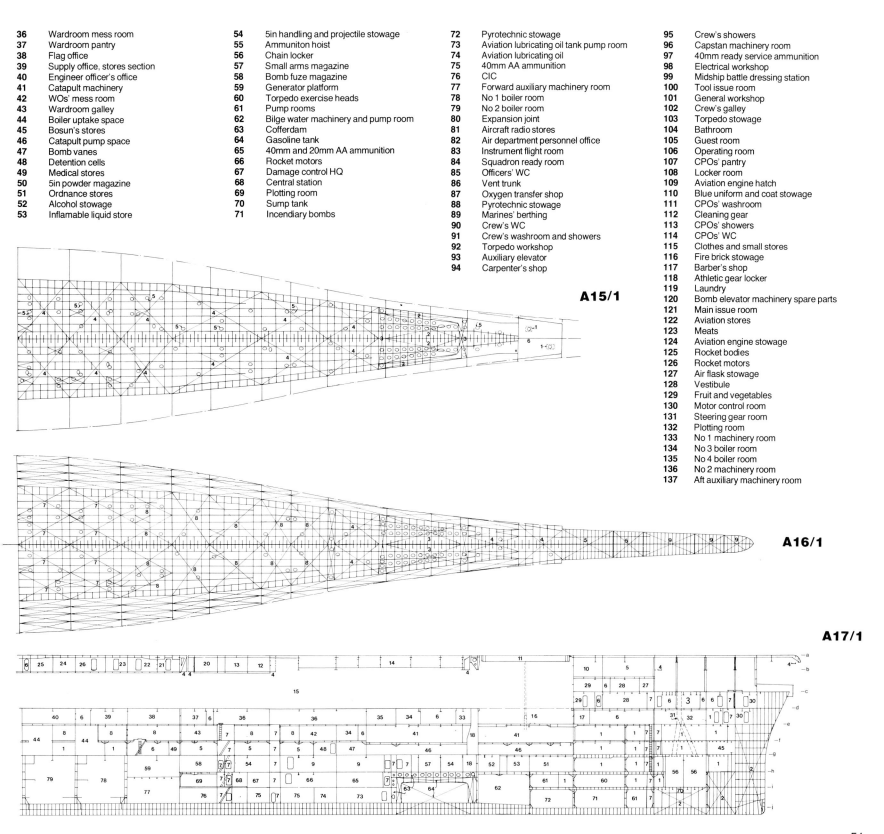

36	Wardroom mess room
37	Wardroom pantry
38	Flag office
39	Supply office, stores section
40	Engineer officer's office
41	Catapult machinery
42	WOs' mess room
43	Wardroom galley
44	Boiler uptake space
45	Bosun's stores
46	Catapult pump space
47	Bomb vanes
48	Detention cells
49	Medical stores
50	5in powder magazine
51	Ordnance stores
52	Alcohol stowage
53	Inflamable liquid store

54	5in handling and projectile stowage
55	Ammuniton hoist
56	Chain locker
57	Small arms magazine
58	Bomb fuze magazine
59	Generator platform
60	Torpedo exercise heads
61	Pump rooms
62	Bilge water machinery and pump room
63	Cofferdam
64	Gasoline tank
65	40mm and 20mm AA ammunition
66	Rocket motors
67	Damage control HQ
68	Central station
69	Plotting room
70	Sump tank
71	Incendiary bombs

72	Pyrotechnic stowage
73	Aviation lubricating oil tank pump room
74	Aviation lubricating oil
75	40mm AA ammunition
76	CIC
77	Forward auxiliary machinery room
78	No 1 boiler room
79	No 2 boiler room
80	Expansion joint
81	Aircraft radio stores
82	Air department personnel office
83	Instrument flight room
84	Squadron ready room
85	Officers' WC
86	Vent trunk
87	Oxygen transfer shop
88	Pyrotechnic stowage
89	Marines' berthing
90	Crew's WC
91	Crew's washroom and showers
92	Torpedo workshop
93	Auxiliary elevator
94	Carpenter's shop

95	Crew's showers
96	Capstan machinery room
97	40mm ready service ammunition
98	Electrical workshop
99	Midship battle dressing station
100	Tool issue room
101	General workshop
102	Crew's galley
103	Torpedo stowage
104	Bathroom
105	Guest room
106	Operating room
107	CPOs' pantry
108	Locker room
109	Aviation engine hatch
110	Blue uniform and coat stowage
111	CPOs' washroom
112	Cleaning gear
113	CPOs' showers
114	CPOs' WC
115	Clothes and small stores
116	Fire brick stowage
117	Barber's shop
118	Athletic gear locker
119	Laundry
120	Bomb elevator machinery spare parts
121	Main issue room
122	Aviation stores
123	Meats
124	Aviation engine stowage
125	Rocket bodies
126	Rocket motors
127	Air flask stowage
128	Vestibule
129	Fruit and vegetables
130	Motor control room
131	Steering gear room
132	Plotting room
133	No 1 machinery room
134	No 3 boiler room
135	No 4 boiler room
136	No 2 machinery room
137	Aft auxiliary machinery room

A15/1

A16/1

A17/1

A General arrangements

A18/1 TRANSVERSE SECTION AT FRAME 114 (looking aft. A18 drawings are 1/300 scale)

1   Oil fuel
2   Void
3   Fresh water
4   Fire room No 3
5   Barber's shop
6   Fire brick stowage
7   Stores
8   Crew's berthing
9   Uptakes
10 Sheet metal shop
11 Hangar space
12 Passage
13 Crew's WC
14 General workshop

A18/2 TRANSVERSE SECTION AT FRAME 49 (looking forward)

1   Stores
2   Passage

3   0.5cal aircraft ammunition magazine
4   Gasoline tank
5   Cofferdam
6   Void
7   Oil fuel
8   Warrant officers' WC
9   Linen locker
10 Wiring trunk
11 Hangar space

A18/3 TRANSVERSE SECTION AT FRAME 175 (looking aft)

1   Crew's showers
2   Passage
3   Crew's berthing
4   Examination room
5   Sterilising and scrub room
6   Operating room
7   Aviation stores
8   Fruit and vegetables
9   Sensitized film storage
10 Void

A18/1

A18/2

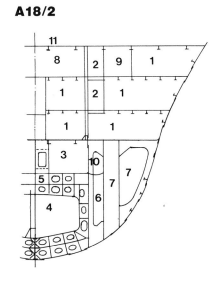

A18/3

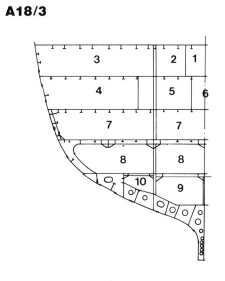

B Hull construction

B1 **MIDSHIP TRANSVERSE SECTION (left side – section at frame 104 looking aft, right side – section at frame 102 looking forward. 1/150 scale)**

1 Armour belt, 4in Class 'B' 10ft deep
2 Water-tight floor
3 Non-tight solid floor (elliptical lightening hole)
4 Stringer, 'T' cut from 'I' girder
5 Longitudinal 'I' girder (flange, welded to deck, of reduced width)
6 Transverse 'T' beam, cut from 'I', with 6in lightening holes
7 Transverse 'I' beam with 6in dia lightening holes
8 Brackets (made from 'I' girders cut to 'T')
9 Stringer, '1' cut from 'I' girder
10 Main deck, two thicknesses of $1\frac{1}{4}$in STS
11 2nd deck, $\frac{1}{4}$in plating (stringer plates $\frac{3}{8}$in HTS)
12 3rd deck, $\frac{1}{4}$in plating (stringer plates $\frac{5}{16}$in HTS)
13 4th deck, $1\frac{1}{2}$in STS
14 Third bottom, $\frac{5}{8}$in plating
15 Inner bottom, $\frac{3}{8}$in plating
16 Outer bottom plating (see B2)
17 'T' stiffener
18 'I' girder, support pillar
19 Pillars
20 Backing bulkheads $\frac{5}{8}$ and $\frac{3}{8}$in plating
21 Holding bulkhead, $1\frac{7}{8}$in STS plating
22 Bracket with 4in flange welded 'on edge'
23 Frame ($\frac{1}{4}$in plating)
24 Bulkhead $\frac{3}{8}$in plating
25 Butt weld
26 Machinery foundation
27 Bilge keel
28 Non-structural bulkheads
29 Longitudinal 'T' cut from 'I' girder, providing upper fixing for torpedo bulkheads
30 Vertical keel
31 'I' frame, supporting holding bulkhead
32 Frame, $\frac{3}{8}$in plating
33 Angle bar connections

B1

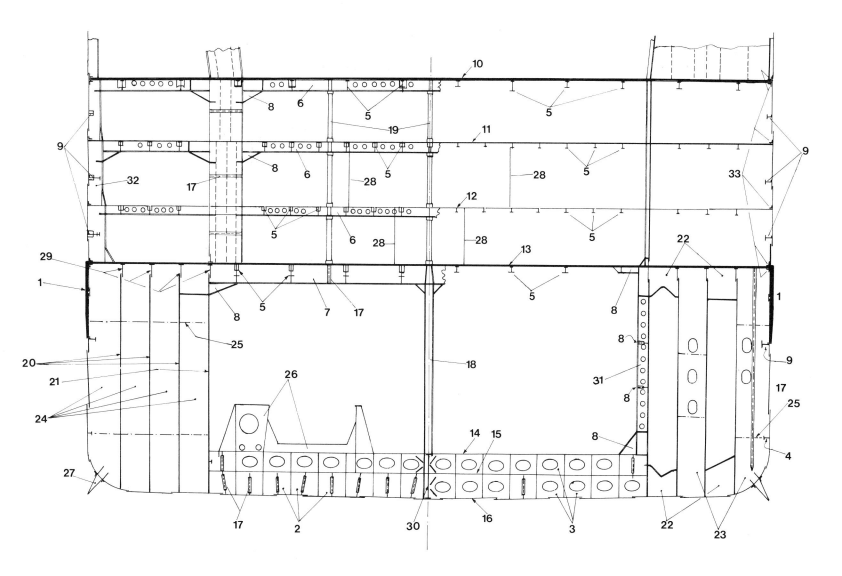

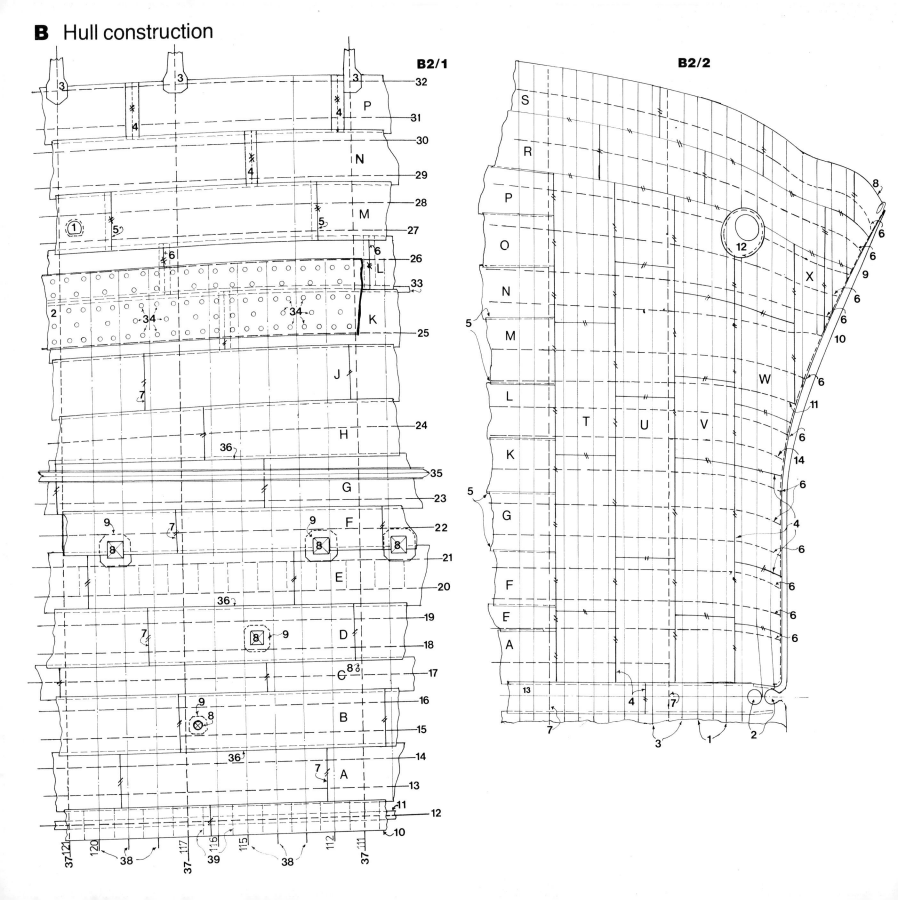

B2/1

B2/2

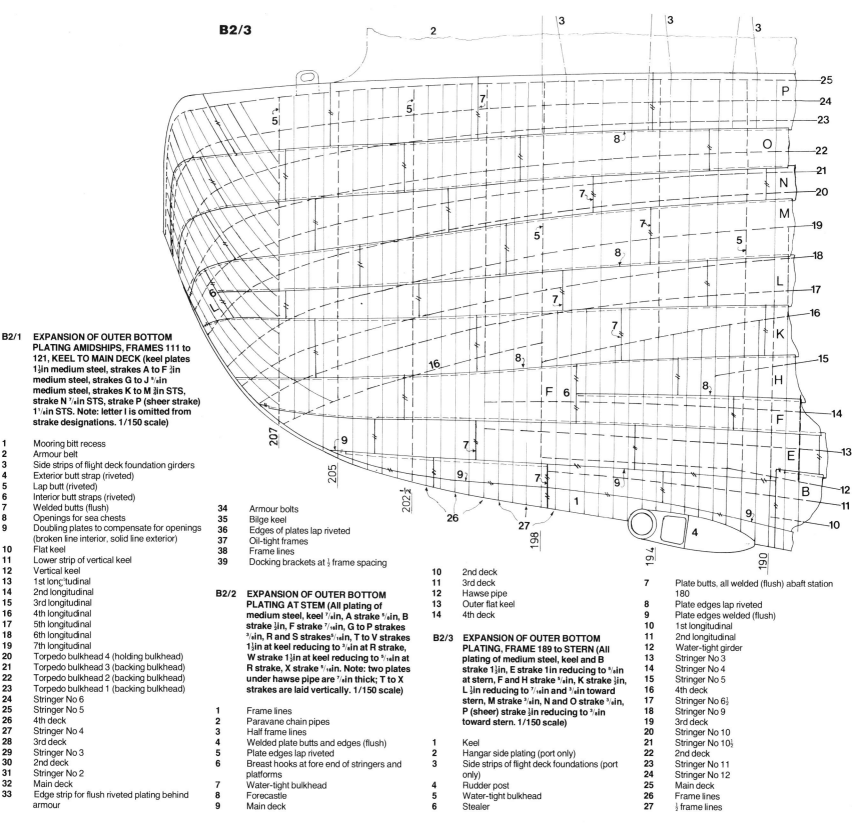

B2/3

B2/1 EXPANSION OF OUTER BOTTOM PLATING AMIDSHIPS, FRAMES 111 to 121, KEEL TO MAIN DECK (keel plates $1\frac{1}{2}$in medium steel, strakes A to F $\frac{3}{4}$in medium steel, strakes G to J $\frac{5}{8}$in medium steel, strakes K to M $\frac{3}{4}$in STS, strake N $\frac{7}{8}$in STS, strake P (sheer strake) $1\frac{1}{8}$in STS. Note: letter I is omitted from strake designations. 1/150 scale)

1	Mooring bitt recess
2	Armour belt
3	Side strips of flight deck foundation girders
4	Exterior butt strap (riveted)
5	Lap butt (riveted)
6	Interior butt straps (riveted)
7	Welded butts (flush)
8	Openings for sea chests
9	Doubling plates to compensate for openings (broken line interior, solid line exterior)
10	Flat keel
11	Lower strip of vertical keel
12	Vertical keel
13	1st longitudinal
14	2nd longitudinal
15	3rd longitudinal
16	4th longitudinal
17	5th longitudinal
18	6th longitudinal
19	7th longitudinal
20	Torpedo bulkhead 4 (holding bulkhead)
21	Torpedo bulkhead 3 (backing bulkhead)
22	Torpedo bulkhead 2 (backing bulkhead)
23	Torpedo bulkhead 1 (backing bulkhead)
24	Stringer No 6
25	Stringer No 5
26	4th deck
27	Stringer No 4
28	3rd deck
29	Stringer No 3
30	2nd deck
31	Stringer No 2
32	Main deck
33	Edge strip for flush riveted plating behind armour

34	Armour bolts
35	Bilge keel
36	Edges of plates lap riveted
37	Oil-tight frames
38	Frame lines
39	Docking brackets at $\frac{1}{2}$ frame spacing

B2/2 EXPANSION OF OUTER BOTTOM PLATING AT STEM (All plating of medium steel, keel $\frac{7}{8}$in, A strake $\frac{5}{8}$in, B strake $\frac{3}{4}$in, F strake $\frac{7}{16}$in, G to P strakes $\frac{3}{8}$in, R and S strakes $\frac{5}{16}$in, T to V strakes $1\frac{1}{2}$in at keel reducing to $\frac{3}{8}$in at R strake, W strake $1\frac{1}{2}$in at keel reducing to $\frac{5}{16}$in at R strake, X strake $\frac{5}{16}$in. Note: two plates under hawse pipe are $\frac{7}{8}$in thick; T to X strakes are laid vertically. 1/150 scale)

1	Frame lines
2	Paravane chain pipes
3	Half frame lines
4	Welded plate butts and edges (flush)
5	Plate edges lap riveted
6	Breast hooks at fore end of stringers and platforms
7	Water-tight bulkhead
8	Forecastle
9	Main deck
10	2nd deck
11	3rd deck
12	Hawse pipe
13	Outer flat keel
14	4th deck

B2/3 EXPANSION OF OUTER BOTTOM PLATING, FRAME 189 to STERN (All plating of medium steel, keel and B strake $1\frac{1}{2}$in reducing to $\frac{5}{8}$in at stern, F and H strake $\frac{5}{8}$in, K strake $\frac{1}{2}$in, L $\frac{1}{2}$in reducing to $\frac{7}{16}$in and $\frac{3}{8}$in toward stern, M strake $\frac{3}{8}$in, N and O strake $\frac{3}{8}$in, P (sheer) strake $\frac{1}{2}$in reducing to $\frac{3}{8}$in toward stern. 1/150 scale)

1	Keel
2	Hangar side plating (port only)
3	Side strips of flight deck foundations (port only)
4	Rudder post
5	Water-tight bulkhead
6	Stealer
7	Plate butts, all welded (flush) abaft station 180
8	Plate edges lap riveted
9	Plate edges welded (flush)
10	1st longitudinal
11	2nd longitudinal
12	Water-tight girder
13	Stringer No 3
14	Stringer No 4
15	Stringer No 5
16	4th deck
17	Stringer No $6\frac{1}{2}$
18	Stringer No 9
19	3rd deck
20	Stringer No 10
21	Stringer No $10\frac{1}{2}$
22	2nd deck
23	Stringer No 11
24	Stringer No 12
25	Main deck
26	Frame lines
27	$\frac{1}{2}$ frame lines

B Hull construction

B3/1

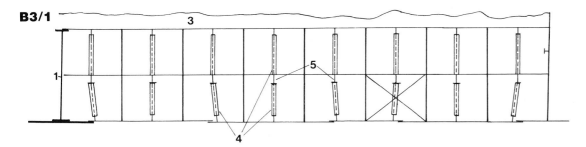

B2/3

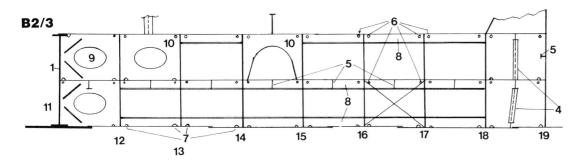

B3/3

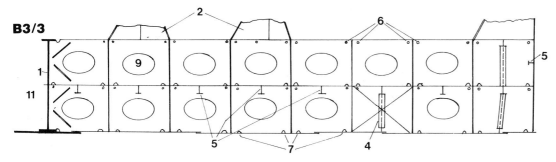

B5

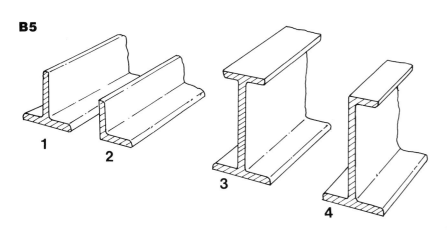

B6

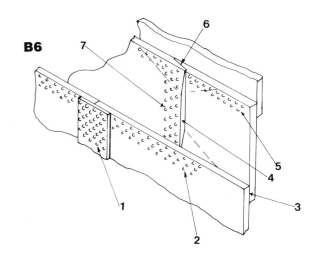

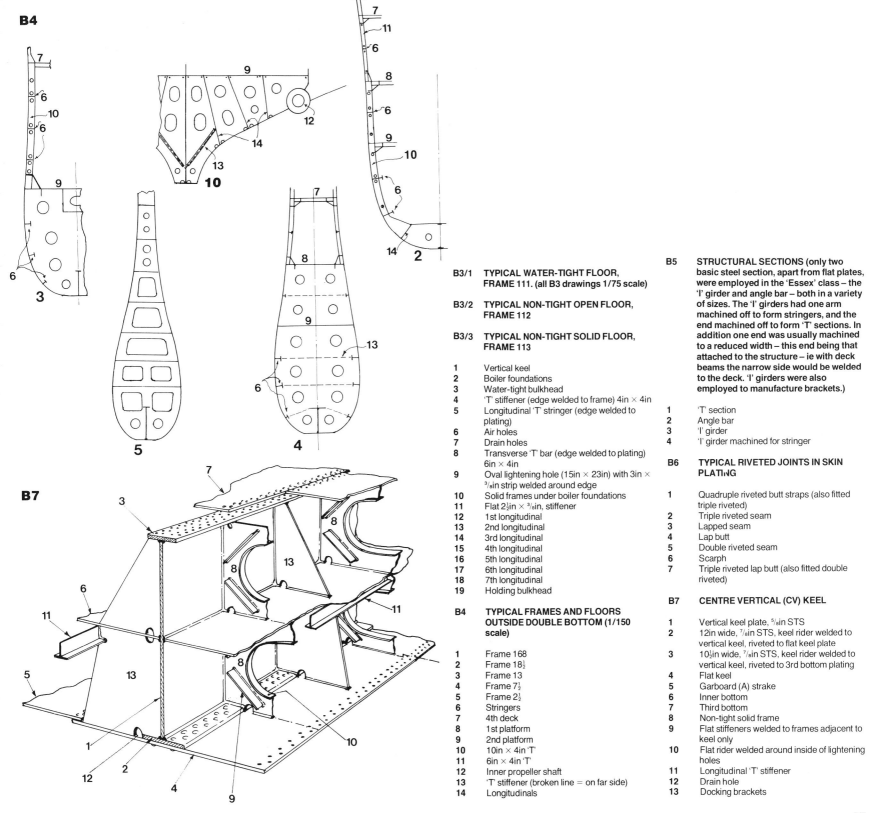

B4

B7

10

3

5

4

2

B3/1 **TYPICAL WATER-TIGHT FLOOR, FRAME 111.** (all B3 drawings 1/75 scale)

B3/2 **TYPICAL NON-TIGHT OPEN FLOOR, FRAME 112**

B3/3 **TYPICAL NON-TIGHT SOLID FLOOR, FRAME 113**

1	Vertical keel
2	Boiler foundations
3	Water-tight bulkhead
4	'T' stiffener (edge welded to frame) 4in × 4in
5	Longitudinal 'T' stringer (edge welded to plating)
6	Air holes
7	Drain holes
8	Transverse 'T' bar (edge welded to plating) 6in × 4in
9	Oval lightening hole (15in × 23in) with 3in × 3/8in strip welded around edge
10	Solid frames under boiler foundations
11	Flat 2½in × 3/8in, stiffener
12	1st longitudinal
13	2nd longitudinal
14	3rd longitudinal
15	4th longitudinal
16	5th longitudinal
17	6th longitudinal
18	7th longitudinal
19	Holding bulkhead

B4 **TYPICAL FRAMES AND FLOORS OUTSIDE DOUBLE BOTTOM (1/150 scale)**

1	Frame 168
2	Frame 18½
3	Frame 13
4	Frame 7½
5	Frame 2½
6	Stringers
7	4th deck
8	1st platform
9	2nd platform
10	10in × 4in 'T'
11	6in × 4in 'T'
12	Inner propeller shaft
13	'T' stiffener (broken line = on far side)
14	Longitudinals

B5 **STRUCTURAL SECTIONS** (only two basic steel section, apart from flat plates, were employed in the 'Essex' class – the 'I' girder and angle bar – both in a variety of sizes. The 'I' girders had one arm machined off to form stringers, and the end machined off to form 'T' sections. In addition one end was usually machined to a reduced width – this end being that attached to the structure – ie with deck beams the narrow side would be welded to the deck. 'I' girders were also employed to manufacture brackets.)

1	'T' section
2	Angle bar
3	'I' girder
4	'I' girder machined for stringer

B6 **TYPICAL RIVETED JOINTS IN SKIN PLATING**

1	Quadruple riveted butt straps (also fitted triple riveted)
2	Triple riveted seam
3	Lapped seam
4	Lap butt
5	Double riveted seam
6	Scarph
7	Triple riveted lap butt (also fitted double riveted)

B7 **CENTRE VERTICAL (CV) KEEL**

1	Vertical keel plate, 5/8in STS
2	12in wide, 7/8in STS, keel rider welded to vertical keel, riveted to flat keel plate
3	10½in wide, 7/8in STS, keel rider welded to vertical keel, riveted to 3rd bottom plating
4	Flat keel
5	Garboard (A) strake
6	Inner bottom
7	Third bottom
8	Non-tight solid frame
9	Flat stiffeners welded to frames adjacent to keel only
10	Flat rider welded around inside of lightening holes
11	Longitudinal 'T' stiffener
12	Drain hole
13	Docking brackets

B Hull construction

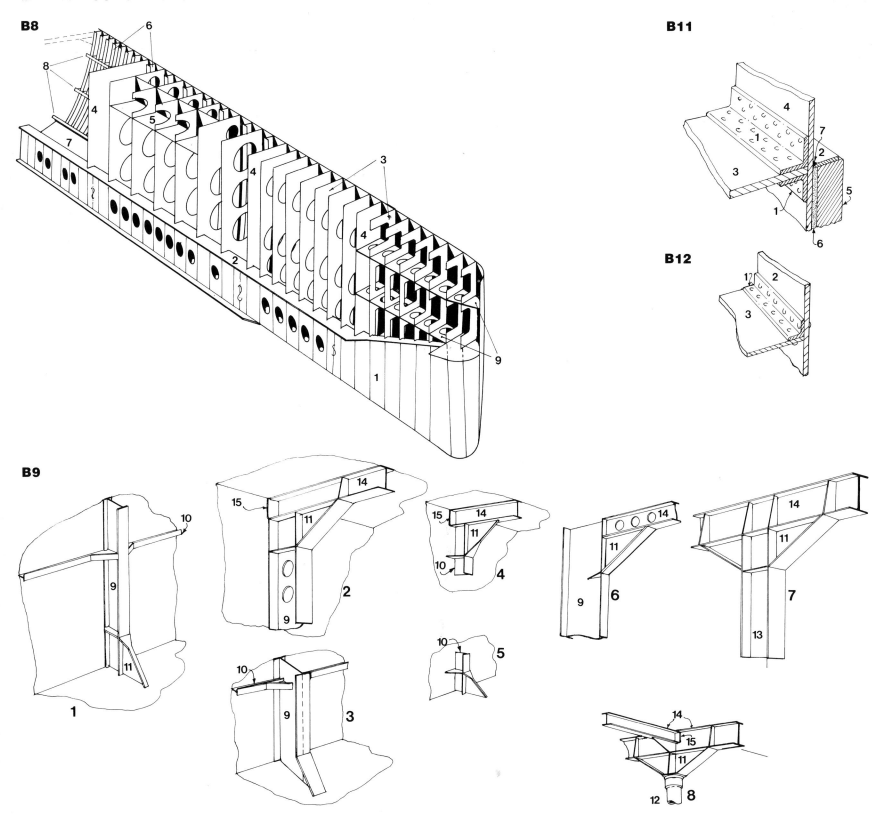

B8

B9

B11

B12

B10

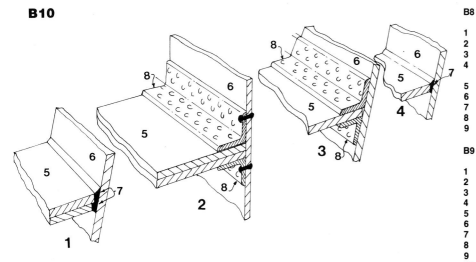

B13

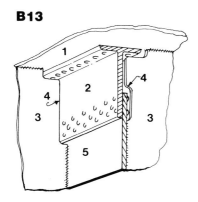

B14

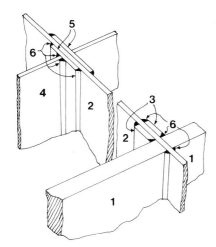

B8   CV KEEL AT STEM

1   CV keel
2   Keel rider
3   Peak tanks
4   Water-tight bulkheads (at stations 4, 8 and 15)
5   Drain tank for cable locker
6   'T' bar frames
7   Platform
8   'T' stringer
9   Breast hooks

B9   TYPICAL BRACKETS

1   Heel of main bulkhead frame
2   Head of main bulkhead frame
3   Heel of side frame
4   Head of minor water-tight bulkhead frame
5   Heel of minor water-tight bulkhead frame
6   Head of side frame
7   Brackets at top of girder pillar
8   Brackets at head of tubular pillar
9   'I' girder frame
10 'T' bar stiffener
11 Bracket (constructed from machined 'I' girder)
12 Tubular pillar
13 Girder pillar
14 'I' girder beam
15 Filling piece welded in gap provided for beam

B10   CONNECTION OF MAIN DECK TO SKIN PLATING

1   Connection at Frames 26–55
2   Connection at Frames 55–166
3   Connection at Frames 166–181
4   Connection forward of frame 26 and aft of frame 181
5   Deck plating
6   Skin plating
7   Weld
8   Double riveted STS angle bar

B11   CONNECTION OF 4TH DECK TO SKIN PLATING

1   Double riveted STS angle bar
2   Fashion plate
3   4th deck plating
4   Skin plating
5   Belt armour
6   Armour backing compound
7   Weld

B12   CONNECTION OF 2nd AND 3rd DECKS TO SKIN PLATING (amidships)

1   Single riveted angle bar
2   Skin plating
3   Deck plating

B13   CONNECTION OF LONGITUDINAL TORPEDO BULKHEADS TO 4th DECK

1   4th deck
2   'T' bar single riveted to deck head, triple riveted to bulkhead
3   Non-tight frames, welded to bulkhead and deck
4   Frame cut away to clear 'T' bar and rivets (non-tight frames, etc, were generally cut

away in this manner in way of structural sections, plating laps, etc)
5   Torpedo bulkhead

B14   CONNECTION OF LONGITUDINAL HOLDING BULKHEAD TO WATER-TIGHT BULKHEADS AND ARMOURED BULKHEADS

1   4in bulkhead armour (at stations 59 and 166)
2   Longitudinal holding bulkhead
3   Flat bar strips to support edges of armour
4   Water-tight bulkhead
5   Flat bar riders on bulkhead ends (wider bar outboard)
6   Welds

B 15/6

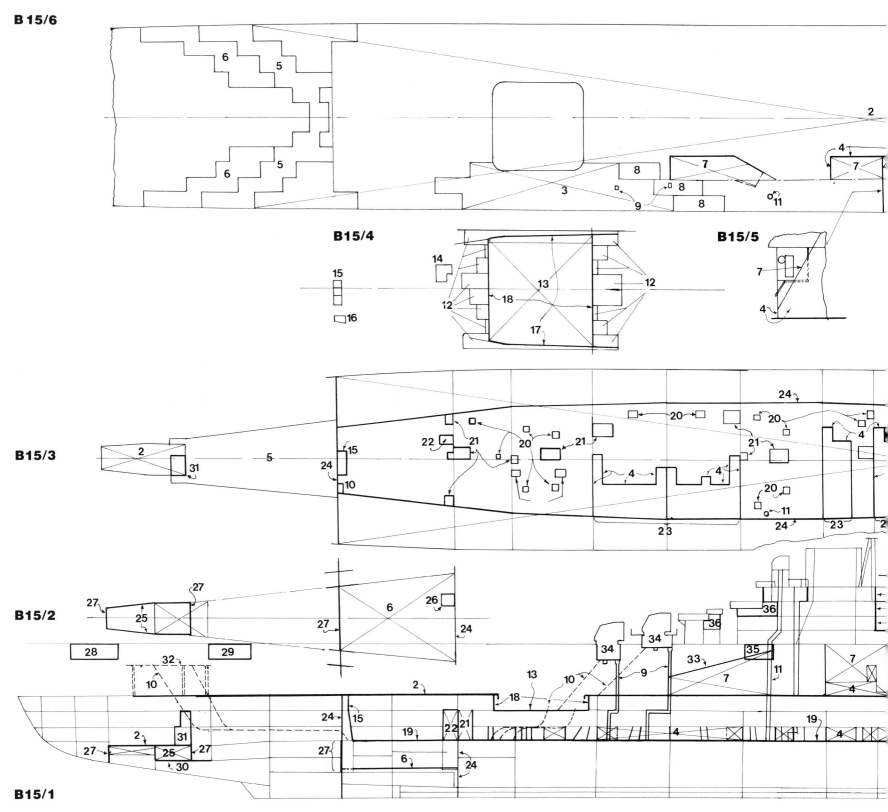

B15/4

B15/5

B15/3

B15/2

B15/1

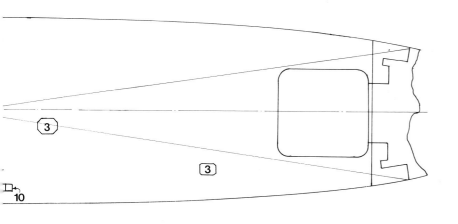

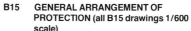

B15   GENERAL ARRANGEMENT OF PROTECTION (all B15 drawings 1/600 scale)

B15/1   PROFILE

B15/2   1st PLATFORM (aft)

B15/3   4th DECK

B15/4   AFT ELEVATOR PIT, 2nd DECK (forward elevator pit similar)

B15/5   SECTION AT SLOPING UPTAKE BULKHEAD

B15/6   MAIN DECK (All plating STS unless otherwise stated)

1	Radio 2, crew shelter and 40mm ready service ammunition, $\frac{3}{4}$in all round
2	$2\frac{1}{2}$in ($1\frac{1}{4} + 1\frac{1}{4}$in) deck
3	$2\frac{3}{4}$in ($1\frac{1}{2} + 1\frac{1}{4}$in) main deck)
4	1in boiler uptakes
5	1in deck
6	$\frac{5}{8}$in deck
7	$1\frac{1}{2}$in sloping bulkhead to boiler uptake
8	$2\frac{5}{8}$in ($1\frac{1}{4} + 1\frac{3}{8}$in) main deck
9	$\frac{3}{4}$in wiring trunk
10	$\frac{3}{4}$in ammunition hoist
11	$\frac{3}{4}$in fire-control tube
12	$\frac{5}{8}$in deck
13	$2\frac{1}{2}$in ($1\frac{7}{8} + \frac{5}{8}$in) deck
14	1in top to bomb elevator
15	1in gas trunk
16	1in ammunition hoist
17	$1\frac{1}{2}$in bulkhead
18	$1\frac{1}{4}$in bulkhead
19	$1\frac{1}{2}$in deck
20	1in vent trunk
21	1in water-tight access trunk
22	1in bomb elevator trunk
23	1in bulkhead
24	$\frac{5}{8}$in bulkhead
25	$4\frac{1}{2}$in Class 'B' armour
26	$\frac{5}{8}$in access trunk
27	4in Class 'B' armour
28	Radio 3, $\frac{3}{4}$in sides, top and bottom
29	40mm ready service and crew shelter $\frac{3}{4}$in sides, top and bottom
30	$\frac{3}{4}$in deck

31	1in air conditioning enclosure
32	Port side gun platform, $\frac{1}{2}$in platform, $\frac{3}{4}$in screens and wiring trunks
33	2in (1 + 1in) boiler uptake
34	5in handling room and mounting, $\frac{3}{4}$in all round
35	Crew shelter, $\frac{3}{4}$in all round
36	Ready service 40mm ammunition, $\frac{3}{4}$in all round
37	Flight deck crew and flight control, $\frac{3}{4}$in all round
38	Radio 1 etc, $\frac{3}{4}$in sides and floor
39	Radar plot, and flag plot $\frac{3}{4}$in sides (radar control 1in side)
40	Pilot house 1in sides, air plot and chart house $\frac{3}{4}$in sides, 2in – 3in roof

Note: Screens to 20mm platforms and 20mm ready service rooms were of $^{3}/_{8}$in STS, those for 40mm guns and bridge screens $\frac{3}{8}$in STS

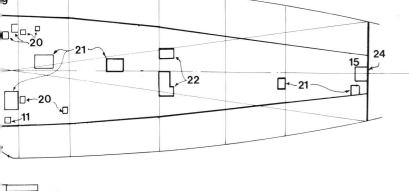

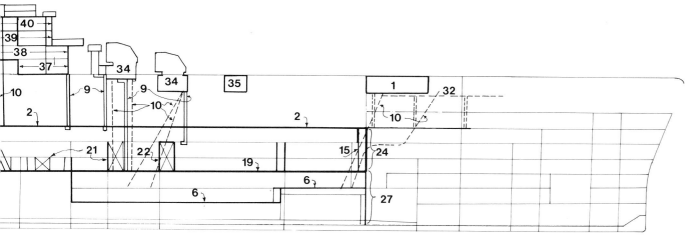

B16

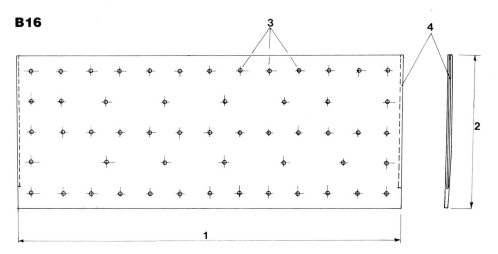

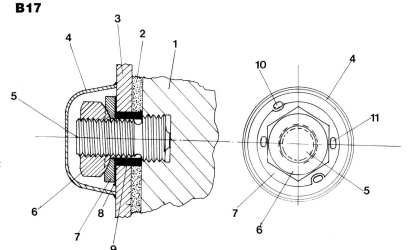

B17

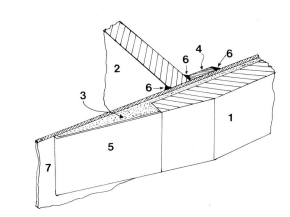

B18

B16	**TYPICAL BELT ARMOUR PLATE (4in Class 'B'. 1/75 scale)**
1	Length 26ft
2	Depth 10ft (maintained as a uniform vertical depth through length of belt hence at ends, where hull was at an angle, actual depth of plate was increased)
3	Position of armour bolt holes
4	Keyways for securing butts of adjacent plates

B17	**BELT, ARMOUR BOLT (no scale)**
1	Armour belt
2	Armour backing compound
3	Skin plating
4	Mild steel cap, welded to skin
5	Nickel steel bolt
6	Nickel steel nut
7	Washer
8	Canvas grommet
9	Stainless steel sleeve
10	Welds to lock washer
11	Welds on washer to lock nut

B18	**SIDE ARMOUR ENDS**
1	Armour belt
2	Armour bulkhead
3	Armour backing compound
4	Flat bar strip to support edge of armour bulkheads
5	Fairwater plate
6	Welds
7	Skin plating

B19	**MIDSHIPS STRUCTURE (at No 3 fire room)**
1	Centre vertical (CV) keel
2	Keel docking brackets (between frames)
3	Outer flat keel
4	Outer bottom (skin) plating
5	1st longitudinal
6	2nd longitudinal
7	3rd longitudinal
8	4th longitudinal
9	5th longitudinal
10	6th longitudinal
11	7th longitudinal
12	Holding bulkhead (plates laid vertically)
13	Holding bulkhead support framing
14	Backing bulkhead No 1 (plates on all backing bulkheads laid vertically)
15	Backing bulkhead No 2
16	Backing bulkhead No 3
17	Support brackets to backing bulkhead (between skin and No 1 bulkhead and No 2 and No 3 bulkheads)
18	Foot and hand holds
19	Vertical 'T' stiffener
20	Brackets in open spaces between torpedo bulkheads
21	Inner bottom plating (laid between longitudinals)
22	3rd bottom plating (laid athwartships abreast main transverse bulkheads and fore and aft elsewhere)
23	Main transverse water-tight bulkhead
24	Water-tight floor (under water-tight bulkhead)
25	Non-tight open floor
26	Non-tight solid floor
27	Transverse deck beam (generally two under each deck per main water-tight section)
28	Longitudinal deck beams
29	4th deck plating (laid fore and aft amidships, laid athwartships between longitudinal bulkheads and sides)
30	3rd deck plating (laid fore and aft)
31	2nd deck plating (laid fore and aft)
32	Main (hangar deck) plating (two courses laid fore and aft)
33	'I' girder pillars (those in engine room on centre line)
34	Pillars
35	Armour belt
36	Frame under flight deck foundation (vertical 'T' stiffeners on side shown, horizontal 'T' stiffeners on far side)
37	Outer bracket of flight deck foundation
38	Stringers
39	Angle bar connections between skin plating and decks
40	Longitudinal bulkhead
41	Hangar side plating (laid vertically)

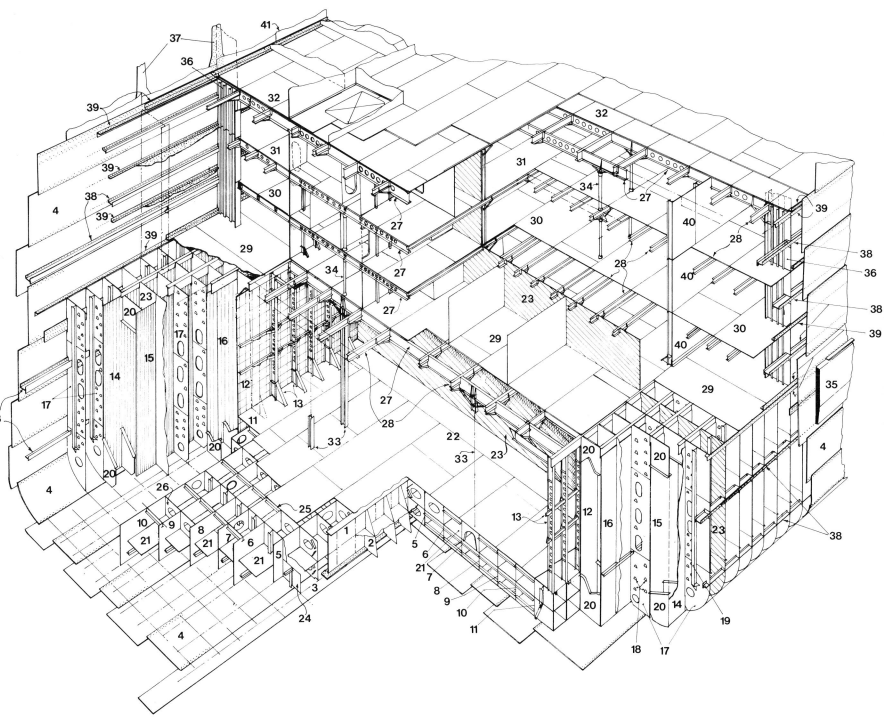

C1

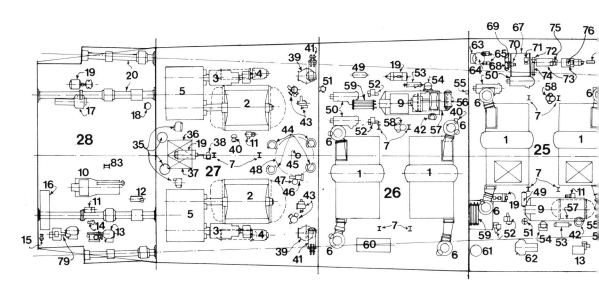

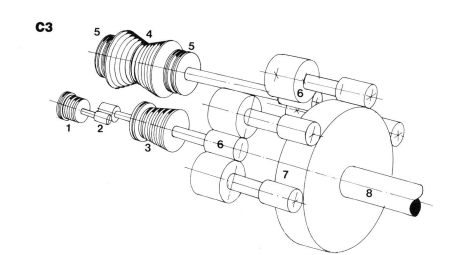

C2

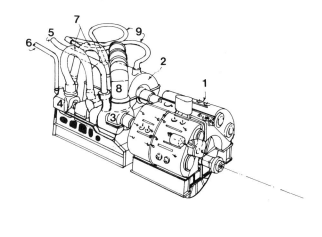

C3

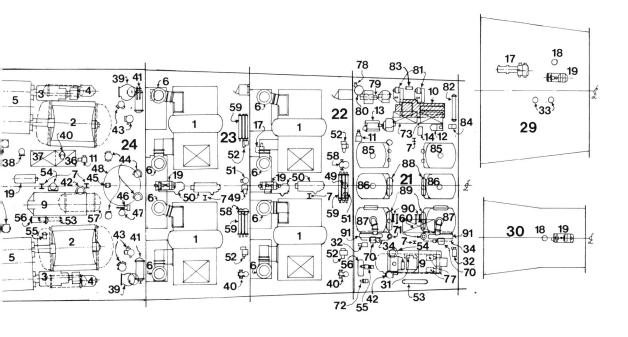

C1	**GENERAL ARRANGEMENT OF MAIN AND AUXILIARY MACHINERY (1/300 scale)**	**33**	Aviation lubricating oil pump		

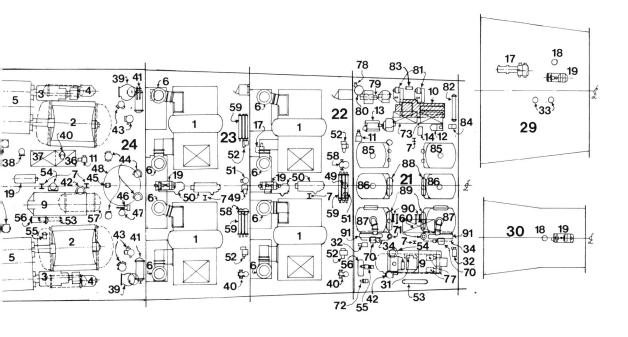

C1   GENERAL ARRANGEMENT OF MAIN AND AUXILIARY MACHINERY (1/300 scale)

1 Boiler
2 Low pressure turbine (main condenser, under)
3 High pressure turbine (main lubricating oil cooler, under)
4 Cruising turbine
5 Gear case
6 Forced draft blower
7 'I' girder pillar
8 Diesel generator cooling water booster pump
9 1250kW turbo-generator
10 250kW diesel generator
11 Auxiliary machinery cooling water pump
12 Diesel fuel oil service pump
13 High pressure air compressor
14 Diesel fuel oil purifier
15 High pressure air compressor cooler
16 High pressure air receiver
17 Fuel oil boost and transfer pump
18 Fuel oil tank drain pump
19 Fire pump
20 Propeller shafts
21 Forward auxiliary machinery room
22 No 1 fire room
23 No 2 fire room
24 No 1 engine room
25 No 3 fire room
26 No 4 fire room
27 No 2 engine room
28 After auxiliary machinery room
29 Fuel oil and damage control pump room (port) aviation lubricating oil pump room (starboard)
30 Forward elevator machinery and pump room
31 Fresh water priming pump
32 Evaporator feed pump

33 Aviation lubricating oil pump
34 Distiller condenser
35 Lubricating oil pumps (2 motor driven, 2 turbine driven in each engine room)
36 Lubricating oil settling tank
37 Lubricating oil storage tank
38 Lubricating oil purifier
39 Main circulating pump
40 Bilge pump
41 Main air ejector
42 Auxiliary condenser pump
43 Main condensate pump (2 motor driven and 3 turbine driven in each engine room)
44 Main feed boost pump
45 Auxiliary feed boost pump
46 Main gland vapour exhauster
47 Gland vapour condenser
48 De-aerating tank
49 Port fuel oil service pump
50 Main feed pump
51 Fuel oil service hand pump
52 Fuel oil service pump
53 Turbo-generator lubricating oil cooler
54 Auxiliary circulating pump
55 Turbo-generator gland vapour exhauster
56 Auxiliary air ejector
57 Auxiliary condenser
58 Emergency feed pump
59 Fuel oil heater (2 in each fire room which, except in No 2 fire room, are mounted one above the other)
60 Ship's service motor generator
61 Low pressure air receiver
62 Low pressure air compressor
63 NTG system air ejector
64 NTG system drain
65 Low pressure drain pump
66 Low pressure
67 Double effect solo shell evaporator
68 Air ejector condenser
69 First effect tube drain pump

70 Distiller circulating pump
71 Distiller condensate pump
72 Distiller fresh water pump
73 Degaussing motor generator
74 Condensate cooler
75 Evaporator brine pump
76 Arc welding set (under) and ship's service fresh water pump (over) degaussing generator
77 Ship's service fresh water pump
78 Medium pressure air compressor cooler
79 Medium pressure air compressor
80 Medium pressure air receiver
81 Air conditioning refrigeration compressor
82 Air conditioning refrigeration condenser
83 Diesel generator circulating water cooler
84 Turbo and diesel generator lubricating oil purifier
85 1st effect evaporator
86 2nd effect evaporator
87 3rd effect evaporator
88 1st stage vapour feed heater
89 2nd stage vapour feed heater
90 Evaporator air ejector
91 Condensate cooler

C2   TURBINE SET

1 Gearcase
2 Low pressure (LP) turbine
3 High pressure (HP) turbine
4 Cruising turbine
5 Main steam to HP turbine
6 Main steam to cruising turbine
7 Exhaust from cruise to HP turbine
8 Exhaust from HP to LP turbines
9 Main steam to astern turbines

C3   DIAGRAMMATIC ARRANGEMENT OF TURBINE SET AND DOUBLE REDUCTION GEARS

1 Cruising turbine
2 Single reduction gear
3 High pressure turbine
4 Low pressure turbine
5 Astern turbines
6 First stage reduction gearing
7 Second stage reduction gearing
8 Output shaft

C Machinery

C4/1

C4/2

C4/3

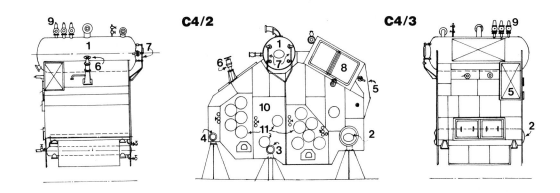

C5/1

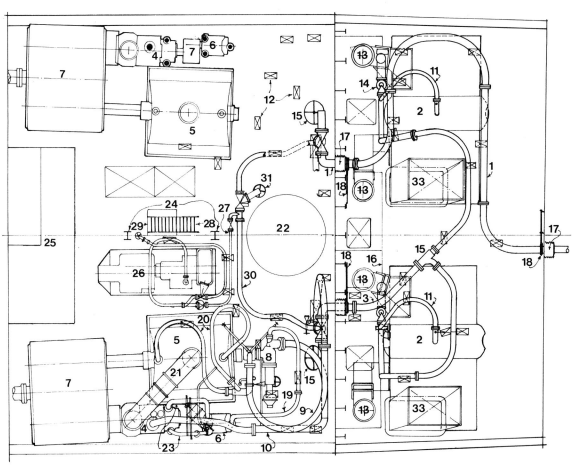

C5/3

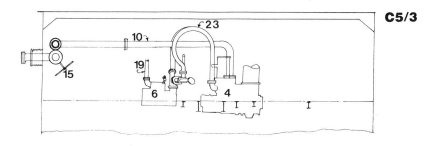

C5/2

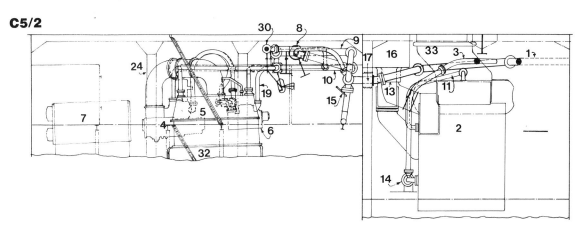

C5/4

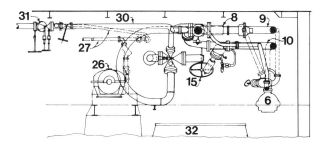

C6

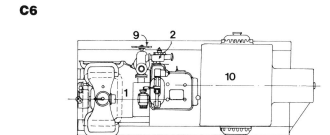

C5/5

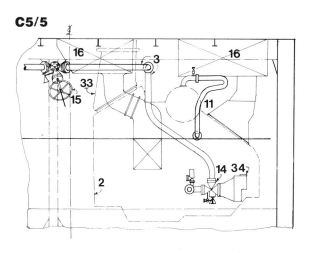

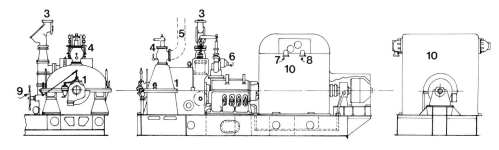

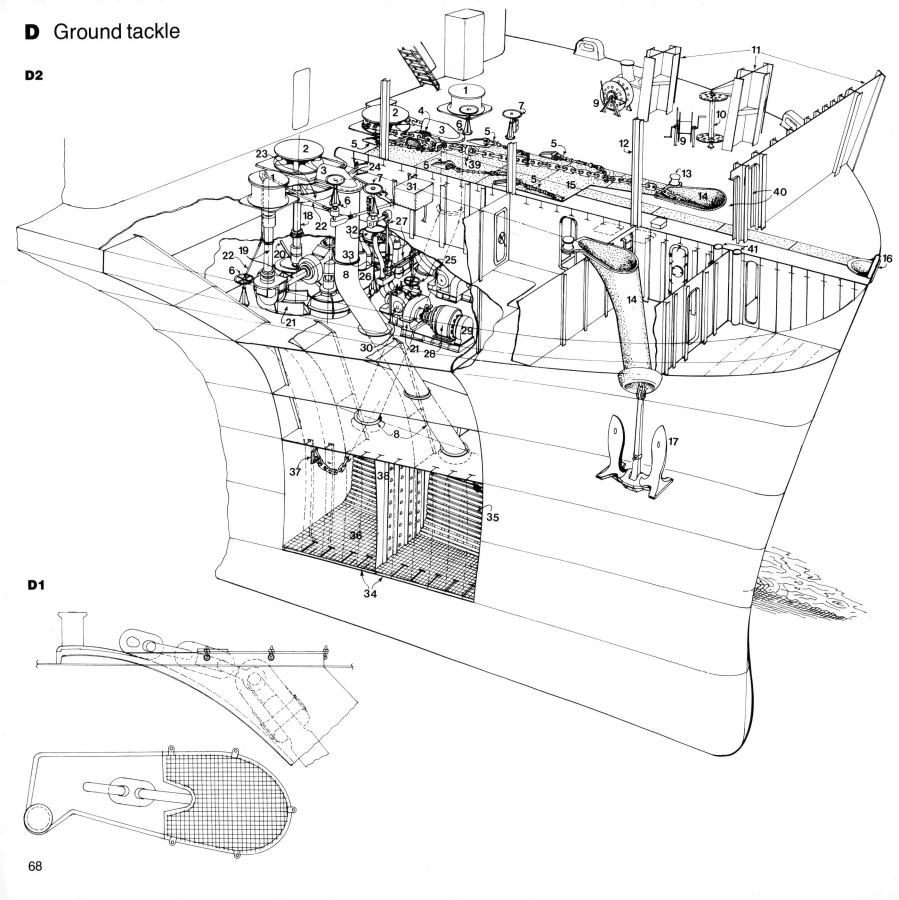

E Superstructure

E1/1

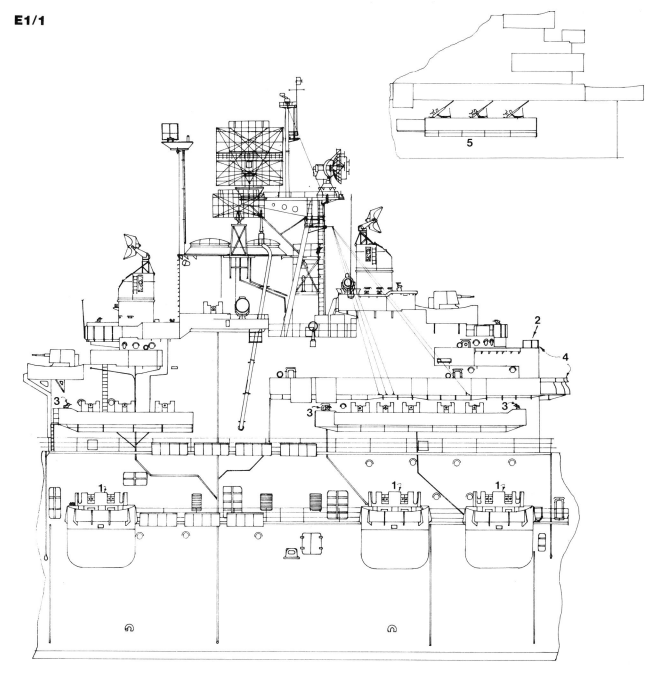

E1/2

E Superstructure

E1/3   **40mm MOUNTINGS ADDED IN PLACE OF CROSS DECK CATAPULT (forward, port side, June 1944)**

E1/4   **ADDITIONAL 40mm MOUNTINGS FITTED ON FANTAIL AND AT PORT SIDE OF FLIGHT DECK AFT**

E1/5   **MODIFICATIONS TO 40mm MOUNTINGS (on starboard side aft)**

1   40mm quadruple mounting added during March–June 1944 refit
2   Forward 40mm mounting on bridge removed during March–June 1944 refit
3   Mk 51 director for 40mm mounting added during March–June 1944 refit
4   Windscreen and wind deflector added to bridge platforms, mid 1944
5   Starboard forward 20mm platform on bridge as completed (for two 20mm added in November 1943 see section A)
6   Mk 51 director added for control of single 5in mounts (also provided on forward platform)
7   20mm platform moved forward to clear new 40mm position
8   Modified stern platform with two 40mm mountings and associate Mk 51 fitted during January–February 1945 refit
9   40mm mounting provided with new sponson mounting mid 1944
10   40mm mounting moved further aft and provided with new sponson mounting, January–February 1945
11   Mk 51 directors moved to gallery deck level, January–February 1945

E1/3

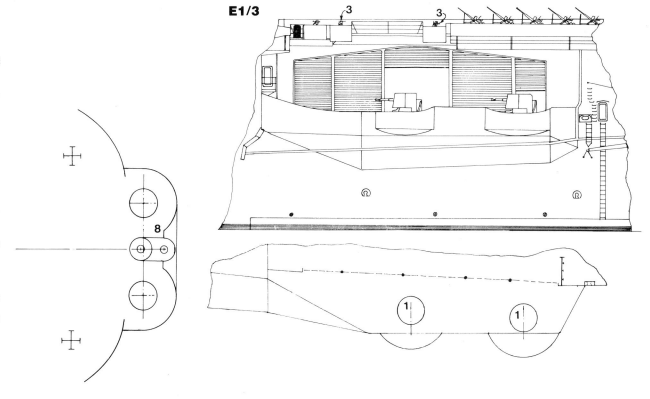

E1/4

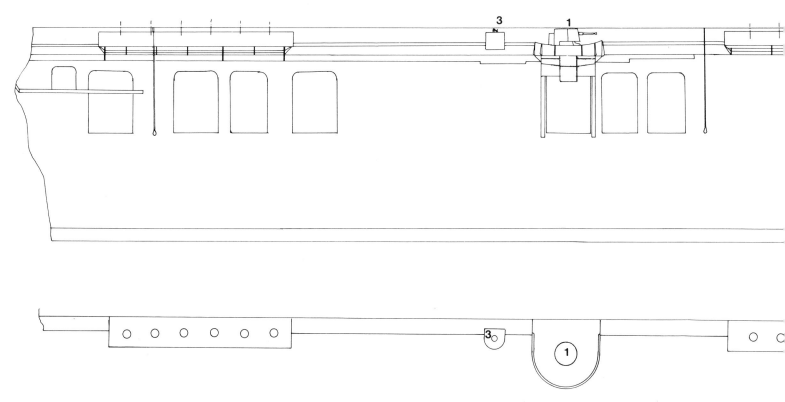

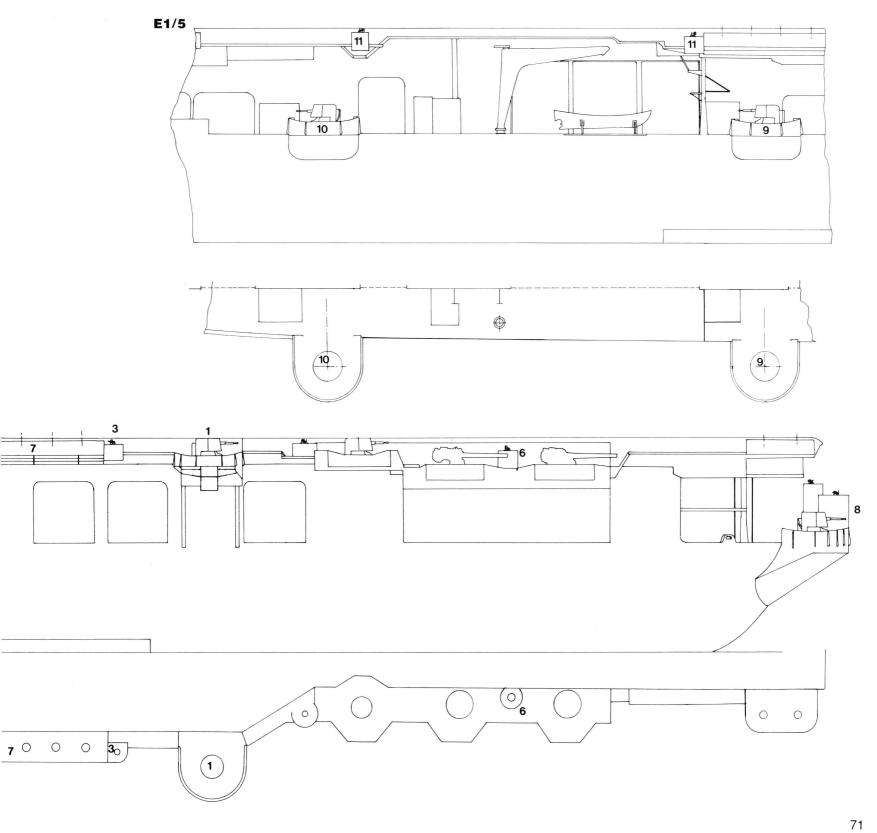

E1/5

E Superstructure

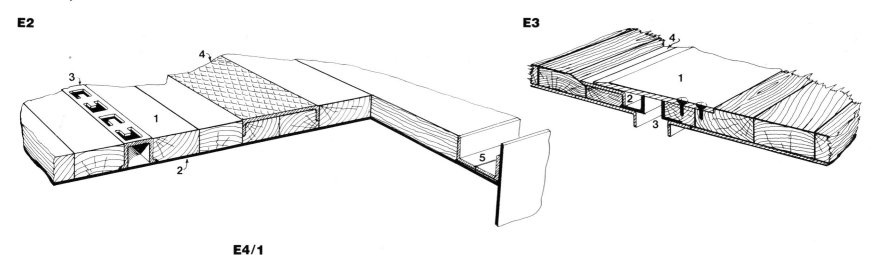

E2

E3

E4/1

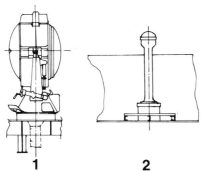
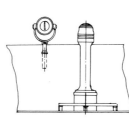
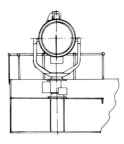
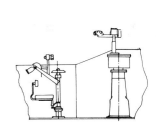

1   **2**   **3**   **4**   **5**   **6**   **7**

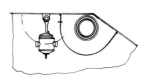
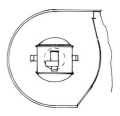
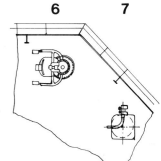

E2 DETAIL OF FLIGHT DECK CONSTRUCTION

1   Wood deck planking
2   Deck plating
3   Aircraft securing rail
4   Arrester wire chaffing plate
5   Waterway at deck edge (those around elevators had covering plates)

E3 DETAIL OF EXPANSION JOINT ON FLIGHT DECK

1   Metal covering plate
2   Waterway
3   Opening
4   Rubbing plate

E4/1 EQUIPMENT ON BRIDGE PLATFORMS (1/75 scale)

1   36in searchlight
2   Pelorus Mk VII
3   12in signalling lamp (on swinging arm attached to screen)
4   Alidade Mk VI (bearing sight)
5   24in searchlight
6   Sky lookout
7   Target designator (transmitter and receiver) Mk 3

E4/2 COMPASS BINNACLE

1   Binnacle hood
2   Sliding cover over compensating magnets (for compass correction)
3   Binnacle stand
4   Electric cable to lamp
5   Hollow iron spheres (for compass correction – adjustable for distance from compass)
6   Compass illuminating lamp

E4/2

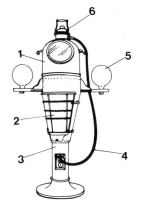

1   Alidade, port and starboard
2   Sky lookouts, port and starboard
3   Target designator, port and starboard
4   Mk 51 director
5   Loudspeaker
6   12in signal lamp, port and starboard
7   Whip antenna
8   TBS antenna
9   BK IFF antenna
10   SG radar antenna
11   SK radar antenna
12   SM radar antenna
13   Mk 37 director
14   Mk 4 radar antenna
15   YE antenna
16   BL IFF antenna
17   Truck light, port and starboard
18   Upper signal yard
19   YE antenna drive unit
20   Repair platform
21   Blinker light, port and starboard
22   Main signal yard
23   Upper fighting lights, port and starboard
24   Speed flag yard
25   Magnetic compass
26   Ship's bell
27   24in searchlight, port and starboard
28   Surface lookouts
29   Siren
30   Siren steam pipe
31   Whistle
32   Whistle steam pipe
33   Steam pipe
34   36in searchlight, port and starboard
35   20mm Oerlikon, port and starboard
36   Intermediate fighting lights, port and
       starboard

37   Lower fighting lights, port and starboard
38   40mm Bofors mounting
39   Wireless antenna, port and starboard
40   Ensign staff
41   Pelorus, port and starboard
42   Pilot house
43   Navigating bridge
44   Primary fly control station
45   Secondary fly control station
46   Flag bridge
47   Flag boards
48   Navigation light, port and starboard
49   Roller curtain to pilot balloon room
50   Flag plot
51   Waterway
52   Expansion joint
53   ECM antenna

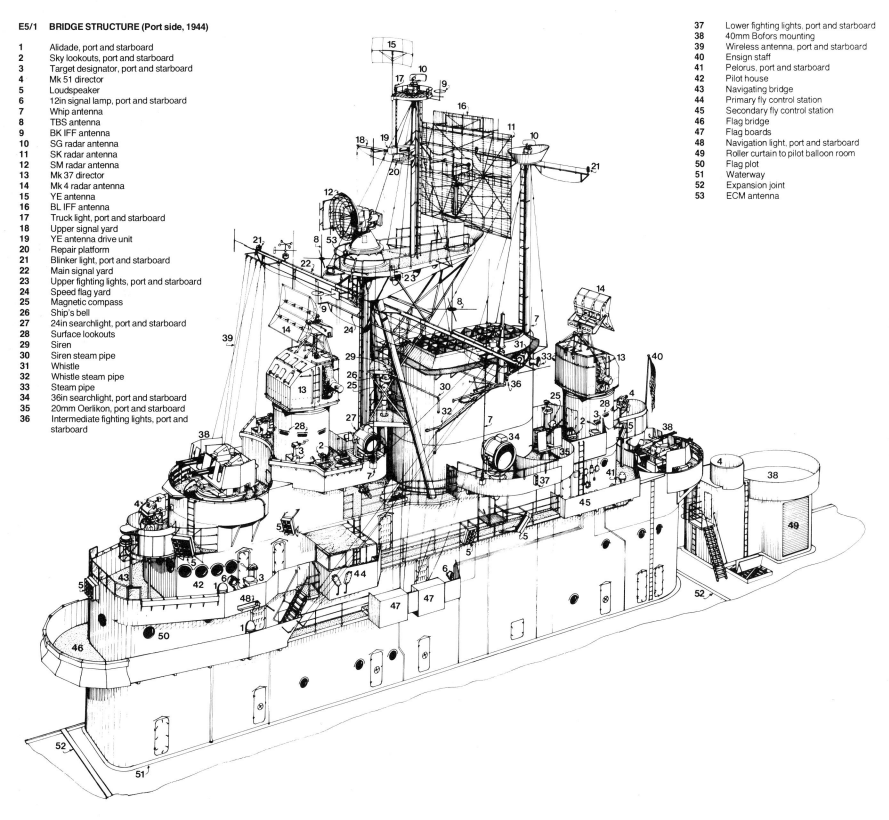

E6

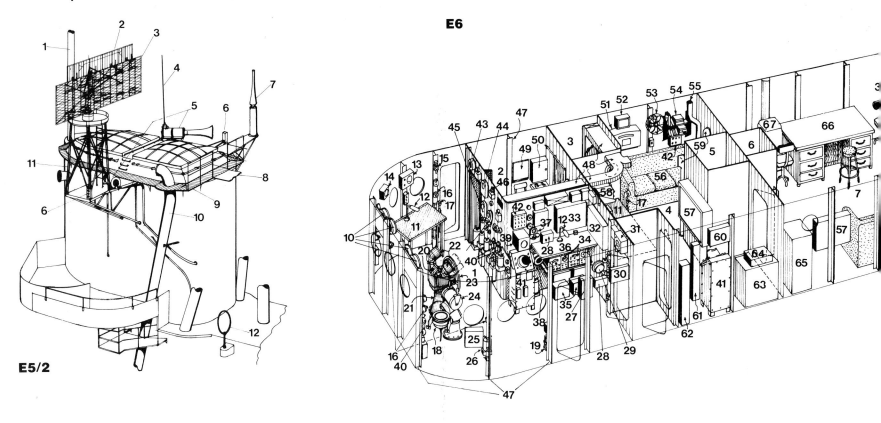

E5/2

E7

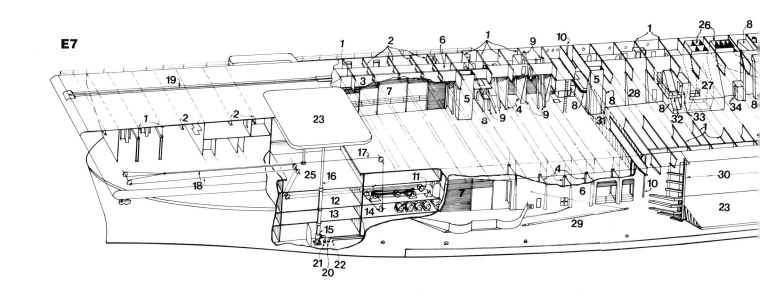

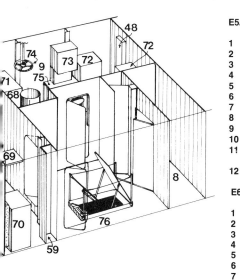

E5/2 STARBOARD SIDE OF STACK (1944)

1 Pole mast on aft end of stack
2 BL-5 IFF antenna (for SC-2)
3 SC-2 radar antenna
4 Whip antenna
5 Whistle (note starboard whistle has no horn)
6 Intermediate fighting lights
7 IFF antenna
8 Walkway to platform on mast
9 Walkway grating around stack top
10 Trash burner stove pipe
11 SC antenna lattice support – shortened during January-February 1945 refit
12 Direction-finder loop antenna

E6 NAVIGATING BRIDGE

1 Pilot house
2 Captain's sea cabin (berth on port side)
3 WC and shower
4 Chart house
5 40mm ammunition hoist
6 Fire-control tube
7 Air plot
8 WC
9 Radar 1
10 Shaft revolution indicators (one per shaft)
11 Chart table
12 Desk light
13 Radar bearing indicator
14 Wind direction and intensity indicator
15 Range indicator
16 Rheostat for window wipers
17 Voice tube
18 Gyro compass repeater, port and starboard
19 Battery lantern, port and starboard
20 Steering telegraph and rudder angle indicator
21 Steering stand
22 Gyro compass repeaters
23 Wheel

24 Engine order telegraph
25 Transmitter reproducer
26 Switch
27 Radio phone unit
28 TBS control box
29 Loudspeaker
30 Supply panel
31 Radio loudspeaker
32 Supply and control panel for running lights
33 Set-up panel for fighting lights
34 Radio receivers
35 Radio receiver power units
36 Radio table
37 Automatic telephone
38 TBS loudspeaker
39 Transmission reproducer
40 Telephone handset
41 Remote PPI unit
42 Running lights supply panel
43 Reproducer
44 Speed and distance indicator
45 Anchor telephone transmission indicator
46 Alarm announcer
47 'T' frames to bulkheads
48 Vent trunk
49 Hinged table
50 Cabinet
51 Recorder amplifier
52 Fighting lights pulsater
53 Fan
54 Book rack
55 Fire main
56 Transom (settee)
57 Dead reckoning tracer
58 Receiver indicator
59 Message tubes
60 Key locker
61 Mercury barometer
62 Rack for rangefinder
63 Instrument locker
64 Chronometer box
65 Filing cabinet

66 Plotting table
67 Teletype receiver
68 Mast
69 Table
70 Safe locker
71 Radar unit
72 Radar transmitter
73 Radio direction-finder set
74 Direction-finder loop antenna training handwheel
75 Direction-finder table
76 Ladderway

E7 GENERAL ARRANGEMENT OF HANGAR

1 Transverse bent (deep girders)
2 Transverse girder
3 Short longitudinal girder in way of hangar side openings
4 Flight deck foundations
5 Bomb elevators
6 Hangar side bulkhead
7 Roller curtain openings in hangar sides
8 Boiler air intake and vent trunks
9 Ammunition hoists
10 Expansion joint
11 Port catapult machinery room (hydraulic ram); on 3rd deck
12 Starboard catapult machinery room; on 3rd deck
13 Starboard catapult machinery pump room; on 4th deck
14 Port catapult machinery pump room; on 4th deck
15 Heel of elevator cylinder; on 1st platform
16 Elevator lifting piston (two to each centreline elevator)
17 Catapult retrieving cable
18 Catapult towing cables
19 Starboard catapult
20 Hydraulic line to No 3 elevator
21 Hydraulic line to No 1 elevator
22 Hydraulic line to auxiliary elevator
23 Aircraft elevator
24 Auxiliary elevator
25 Elevator pit (2nd deck)
26 Boiler uptakes
27 Boiler uptake casing
28 Sloping bulkhead
29 Boat and aircraft boom
30 Deck edge elevator guides
31 Hangar fire curtains
32 Observation and control platform
33 Hangar deck conflagration station
34 Hangar sprinkling control station
35 Repair locker
36 Torpedo hatch
37 Aircraft engine hatch
38 Torpedo elevator
39 Main air vent trunk to longitudinal air trunk on second deck
40 Aviation repair shop

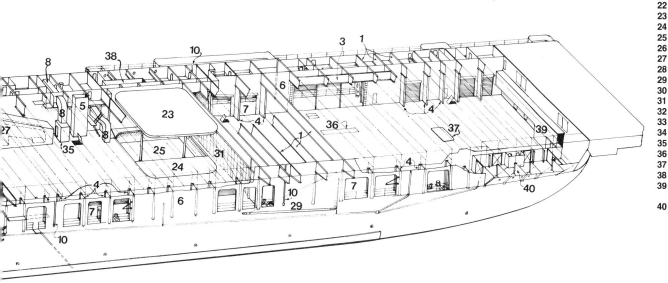

F Rig

F1   FOREMAST, LOOKING AFT (1944. Radar aerials on main platform omitted for clarity. 1/300 scale)

1 YE antenna
2 BK antenna (IFF responder for SG radar)
3 Signal yard, added c July 1944
4 Upper fighting lights
5 TBS antenna
6 Main signal yard
7 Yard stay
8 Anemometer and wind vane
9 Blinker light
10 Truck lights
11 Speed flag yard
12 Signal halyards
13 Wireless antennas
14 Speed cone halyards

F2   MAIN SIGNAL YARD (1944)

1 BK antenna (IFF responder for SG radar, port and starboard)
2 TBS antenna, port and starboard
3 Anemometer and wind vane, port and starboard
4 Access platform
5 W/T antenna, port and starboard
6 Antenna spreader, port and starboard
7 Signal halyards, port and starboard
8 Speed cone halyard, port and starboard
9 Footropes, port and starboard
10 Blinker light, port and starboard
11 Ladder to masthead platform
12 Yard stays
13 Speed flag yard

F3   RADAR RIG (1943–45. All F3 drawings 1/300 scale)

F3/1   AS COMPLETED 1943

F3/2   NOVEMBER 1943 – JANUARY 1944

F3/3   MAY 1944 – 1945

1 YE antenna
2 SK antenna
3 SG antenna
4 SC antenna
5 Signal yard
6 SM antenna
7 YJ antenna (fitted c January 1944, removed c July 1944)
8 Speed flag yard
9 Upper fighting lights
10 SC antenna and platform lowered February 1945
11 Antenna of IFF interrogator for SG radar

F4   SK ANTENNA ARRAY (1/150 scale)

F4/1   PROFILE

F4/2   REAR AND PLAN VIEW OF SUPPORT FRAMEWORK

F4/3   FRONT VIEW OF REFLECTOR FRAME
(Note that mesh behind IFF dipoles is finer than shown – to scale this would fill-in on printing – and that reflector wires are more closely spaced the closer they are to a dipole)

F4/4   ARRANGEMENT OF DIPOLES

1 Twenty-four SK dipoles (6 × 6)
2 Mk 3 (BL-5) IFF dipoles
3 Mk 4 (BG) IFF dipoles (alternative to Mk 3)

F5   SG RADAR ANTENNA (1/150 scale)

F5/1   PROFILE

F5/2   PLAN

F5/3   FRONT VIEW

1 Waveguide
2 Reflector

F6   SC-2 RADAR ANTENNA (1/150 scale)

F6/1   REAR VIEW OF SUPPORTING STRUCTURE

F6/2   PLAN

F6/3   FRONT VIEW OF REFLECTOR

F6/4   FRONT VIEW OF DIPOLES

F6/5   PROFILE

1 SC radar dipoles
2 Mk 3 IFF dipoles
3 Mk 4 IFF dipoles

F7   SM-1 RADAR ANTENNA (no scale)

1 Reflector
2 Mk 3 IFF antenna (BO)

F8   YE AIRCRAFT HOMING BEACON ANTENNA (1/150 scale)

F8/1   PROFILE

F8/2   PLAN

F8/3   FRONT VIEW

F9   SIDE LADDER (1/150 scale)

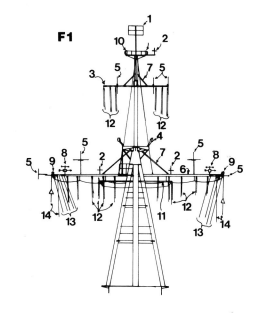

F1

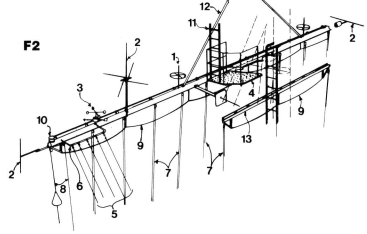

F2

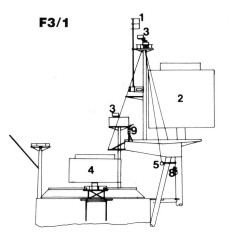

F3/1

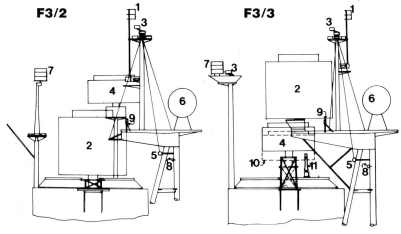

F3/2

F3/3

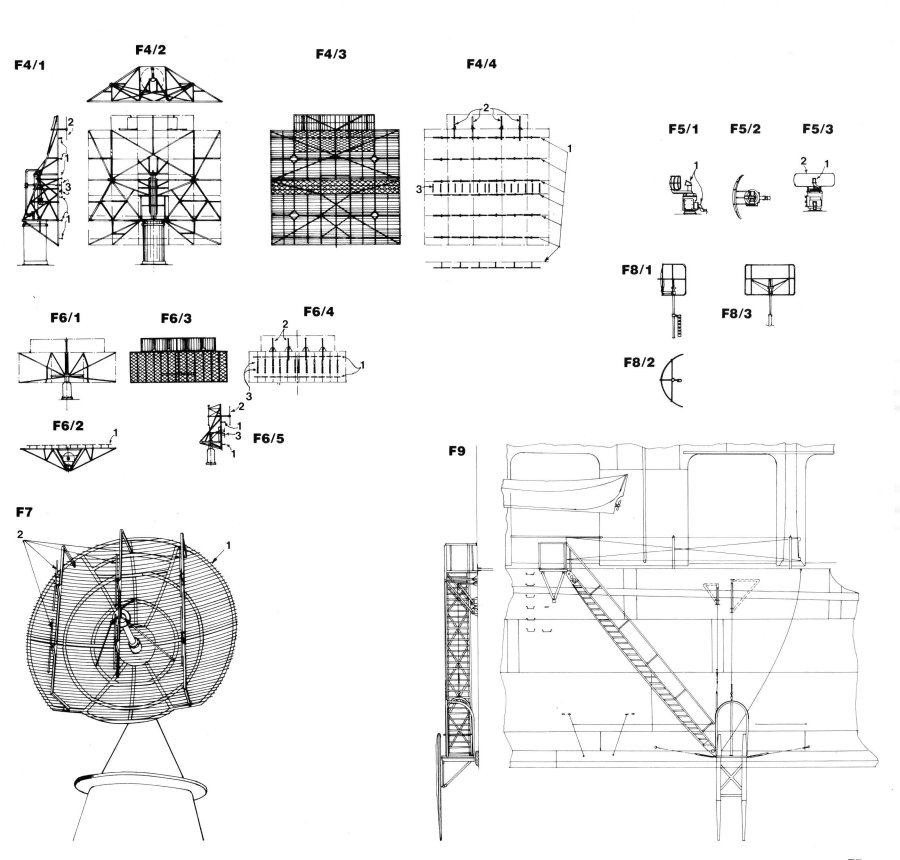

F4/1

F4/2

F4/3

F4/4

F5/1   **F5/2**   **F5/3**

F8/1

F8/3

F6/1

F6/3

F6/4

F8/2

F6/2

F6/5

F7

F9

F Rig

F10   BOAT BOOM (port, aft)

1   Jacobs ladder
2   Guy
3   Lifeline
4   Topping lift

F11   LONG RANGE WIRELESS RIG (1/300 scale. Forward rig illustrated – after rig same but reversed)

1   Antenna spreader
2   Antenna down-leads screen
3   Position of wireless masts when hinged down
4   Insulators
5   Main 'flat top' antenna wires
6   Ladder (on inboard side of mast)
7   Flight deck
8   Antenna lead trunks
9   Stays on near side, far side stays are laid on opposite diagonal

F10

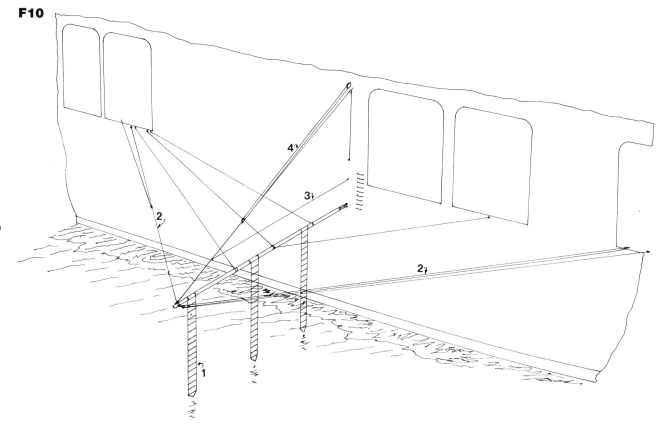

F11

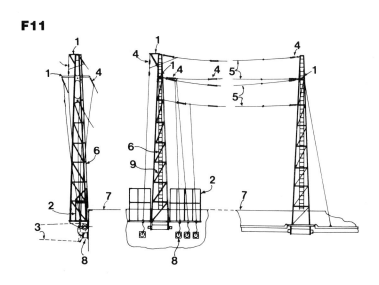

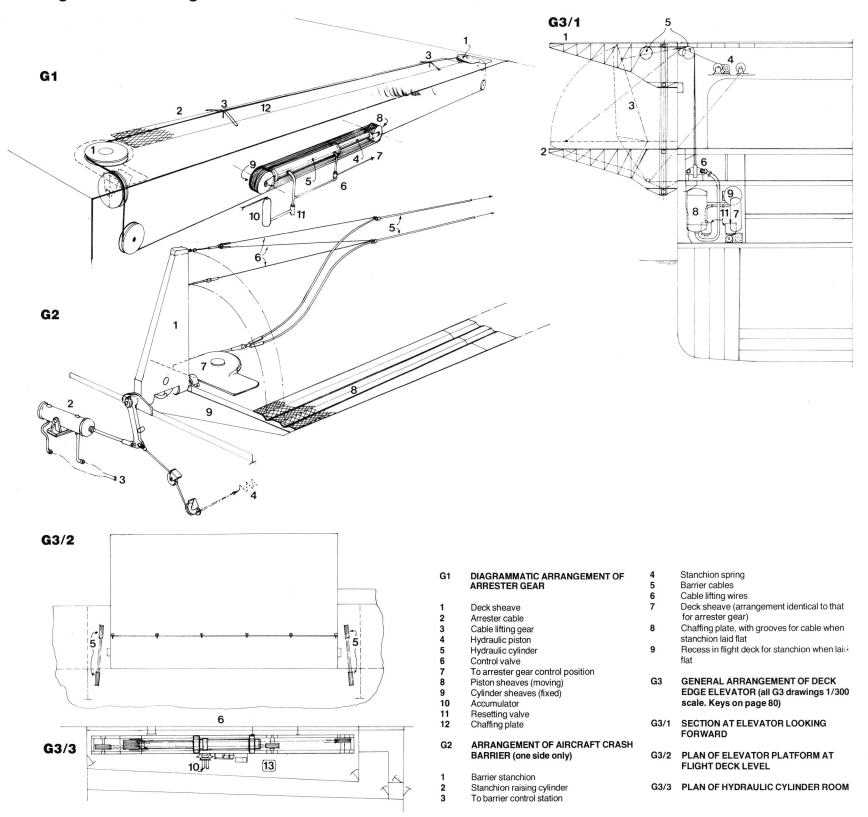

G Flight deck arrangements

G1

G2

G3/1

G3/2

G3/3

G1	**DIAGRAMMATIC ARRANGEMENT OF ARRESTER GEAR**	**4**	Stanchion spring
		5	Barrier cables
1	Deck sheave	**6**	Cable lifting wires
2	Arrester cable	**7**	Deck sheave (arrangement identical to that for arrester gear)
3	Cable lifting gear		
4	Hydraulic piston	**8**	Chaffing plate, with grooves for cable when stanchion laid flat
5	Hydraulic cylinder		
6	Control valve	**9**	Recess in flight deck for stanchion when laid flat
7	To arrester gear control position		
8	Piston sheaves (moving)		
9	Cylinder sheaves (fixed)	**G3**	**GENERAL ARRANGEMENT OF DECK EDGE ELEVATOR (all G3 drawings 1/300 scale. Keys on page 80)**
10	Accumulator		
11	Resetting valve		
12	Chaffing plate	**G3/1**	**SECTION AT ELEVATOR LOOKING FORWARD**
G2	**ARRANGEMENT OF AIRCRAFT CRASH BARRIER (one side only)**		
		G3/2	**PLAN OF ELEVATOR PLATFORM AT FLIGHT DECK LEVEL**
1	Barrier stanchion		
2	Stanchion raising cylinder	**G3/3**	**PLAN OF HYDRAULIC CYLINDER ROOM**
3	To barrier control station		

G Flight deck arrangements

G3/4 PLAN OF ELEVATOR MACHINERY ROOM AT 3rd DECK LEVEL

G3/5 PLAN OF ELEVATOR MACHINERY ROOM AT 4th DECK LEVEL

1 Platform (raised position)
2 Platform (lowered position)
3 Platform (hinged position)
4 Platform hinge winch
5 Upper platform-lifting sheaves
6 Hydraulic lifting cylinder
7 Storage tank
8 Expansion tank
9 Pressure tank
10 Control valves
11 Main hydraulic pumps
12 Gratings
13 Ladder

G4 PORTABLE PALLISADE (1/37.5 scale)

1 Channel frame with lightening holes
2 Handle
3 Locking pin
4 Deck latch

G5 FLIGHT DECK LAYOUT (1944. 1/1200 scale)

1 Aircraft outrigger
2 Arrester wires
3 Catapult
4 Bomb elevator
5 Hinged canvas wind shield to signal platform
6 Barriers
7 Gasoline station
8 Arrester gear control station
9 Barrier control station (one to each barrier)
10 Signal platform (position for landing signals officer – LSO)
11 No 1 elevator
12 No 2 (deck edge) elevator
13 No 3 elevator
14 Flight deck ramps
15 Torpedo elevator
16 Welding elements (arrester wire lifting springs)

G6 FLIGHT DECK GASOLINE STATION (note: those on the hangar deck were generally similar)

1 Filter
2 Syphon
3 Connection for 75ft filling hose
4 Aircraft degassing connection
5 Gallery deck walkway
6 Flush hinged cover to hose tubs
7 Flight deck
8 Main gasoline pipe

G3/4

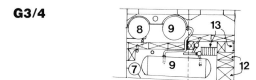

G4

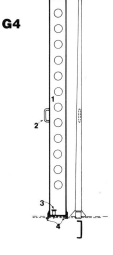

G3/5

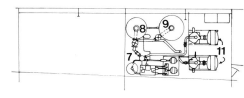

G6

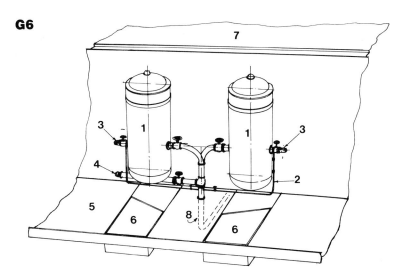

G5

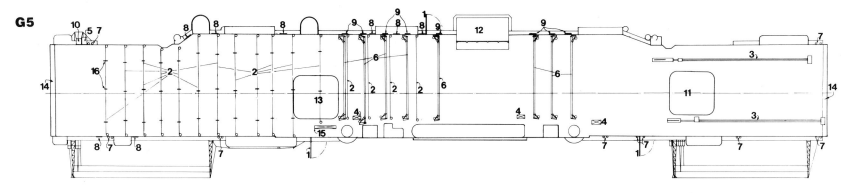

80

H Aircraft

H1 CURTIS HELLDIVER (SB2C)

H2 GRUMMAN HELLCAT (F6F-3). 1/150
scale

H3 GRUMMAN AVENGER (TBF1). 1/150
scale

H2

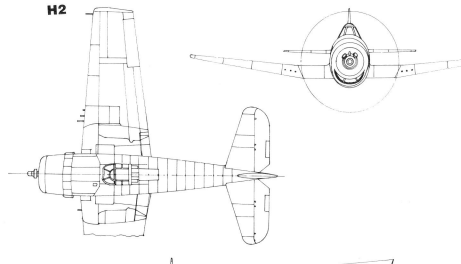

H1

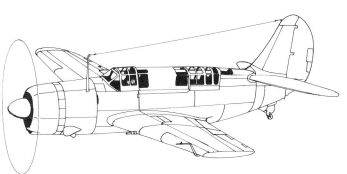

H3

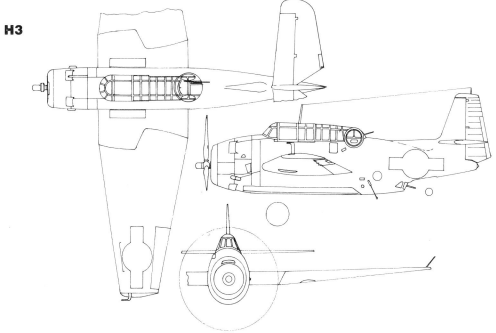

H4

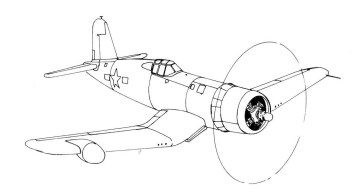

H5

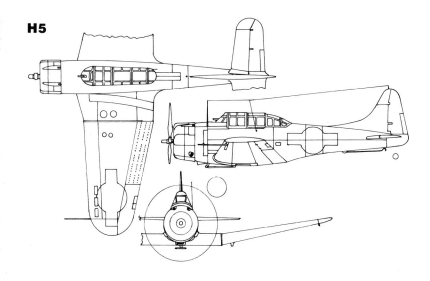

H4   **CHANCE VOUGHT CORSAIR (F4U)**

H5   **DOUGLAS DAUNTLESS (SBD3). 1/150
scale**

I Armament

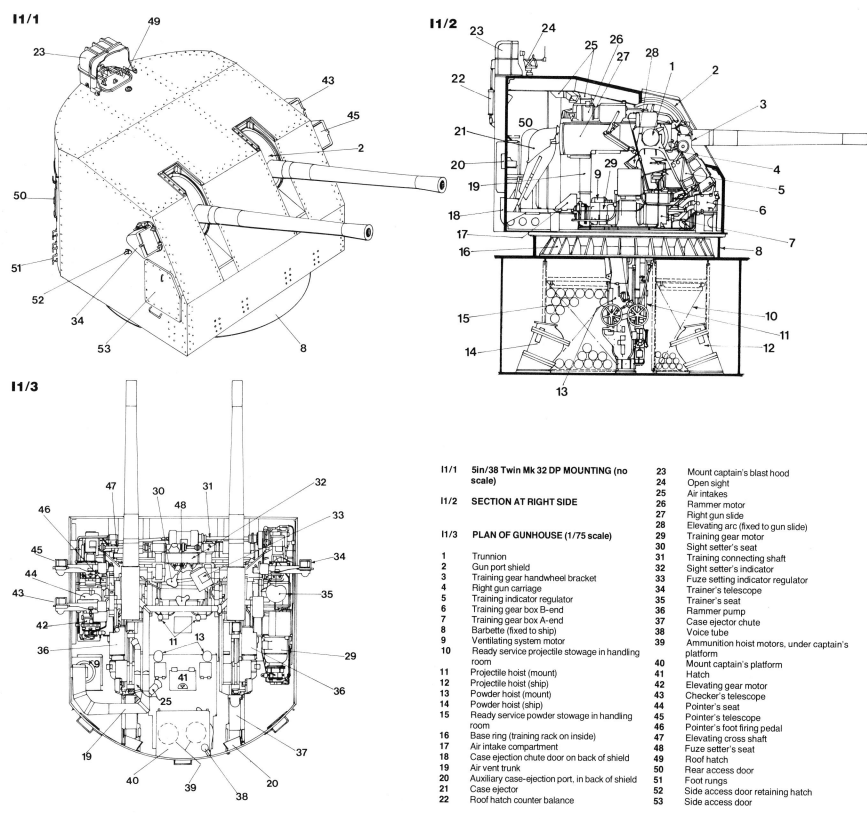

I1/1

I1/2

I1/3

I1/1	5in/38 Twin Mk 32 DP MOUNTING (no scale)	23	Mount captain's blast hood
		24	Open sight
		25	Air intakes
I1/2	**SECTION AT RIGHT SIDE**	26	Rammer motor
		27	Right gun slide
		28	Elevating arc (fixed to gun slide)
I1/3	**PLAN OF GUNHOUSE (1/75 scale)**	29	Training gear motor
		30	Sight setter's seat
1	Trunnion	31	Training connecting shaft
2	Gun port shield	32	Sight setter's indicator
3	Training gear handwheel bracket	33	Fuze setting indicator regulator
4	Right gun carriage	34	Trainer's telescope
5	Training indicator regulator	35	Trainer's seat
6	Training gear box B-end	36	Rammer pump
7	Training gear box A-end	37	Case ejector chute
8	Barbette (fixed to ship)	38	Voice tube
9	Ventilating system motor	39	Ammunition hoist motors, under captain's platform
10	Ready service projectile stowage in handling room	40	Mount captain's platform
11	Projectile hoist (mount)	41	Hatch
12	Projectile hoist (ship)	42	Elevating gear motor
13	Powder hoist (mount)	43	Checker's telescope
14	Powder hoist (ship)	44	Pointer's seat
15	Ready service powder stowage in handling room	45	Pointer's telescope
16	Base ring (training rack on inside)	46	Pointer's foot firing pedal
17	Air intake compartment	47	Elevating cross shaft
18	Case ejection chute door on back of shield	48	Fuze setter's seat
19	Air vent trunk	49	Roof hatch
20	Auxiliary case-ejection port, in back of shield	50	Rear access door
21	Case ejector	51	Foot rungs
22	Roof hatch counter balance	52	Side access door retaining hatch
		53	Side access door

I2/1

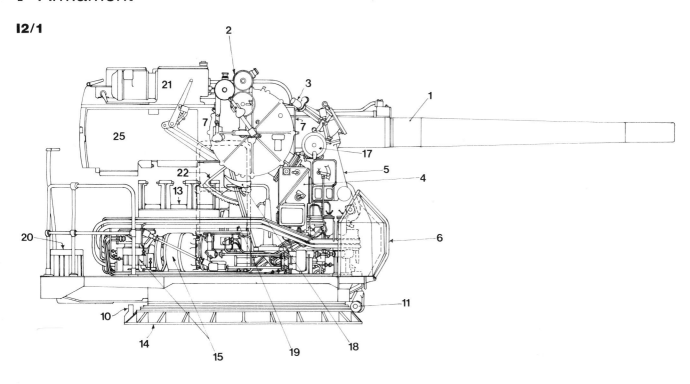

I2/2

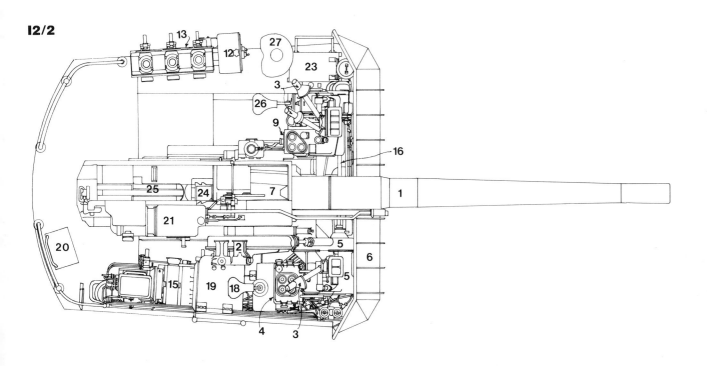

I2/3

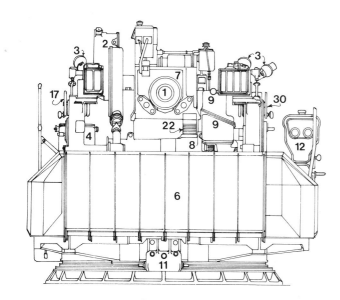

1	5in Mk 12 gun
2	Sight setting gear
3	Telescopes
4	Gun training indicator regulator
5	Training gear
6	Spray shield
7	Gun slide
8	Elevating gear
9	Gun elevating indicator regulator
10	Training stop
11	Training buffer
12	Fuze setting indicator regulator
13	Fuze setting machine
14	Stand
15	Electro-hydraulic training motor
16	Elevating cross shaft
17	Training crank
18	Trainer's seat
19	Sight setter's platform
20	Loading platform
21	Rammer pump
22	Elevating arc
23	Checker's platform
24	Breech block
25	Rammer
26	Pointer's seat
27	Fuze setter's seat
28	Trunnion
29	Trunnion bracket
30	Elevating crank

I2/4

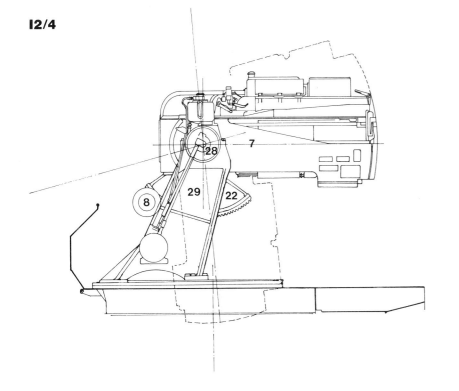

I2/5

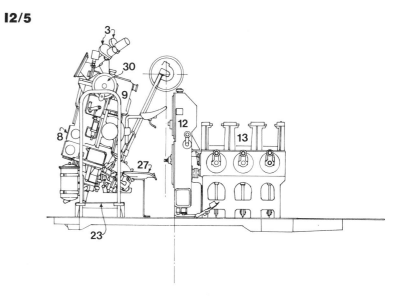

I3/1

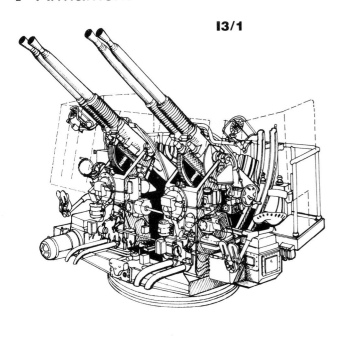

I3/2

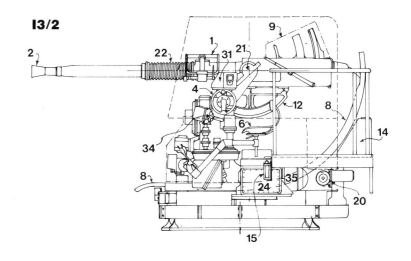

I3/3

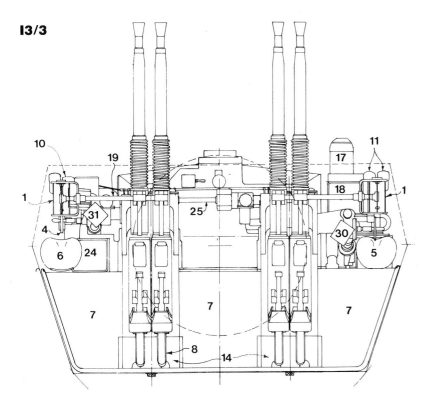

I3/4

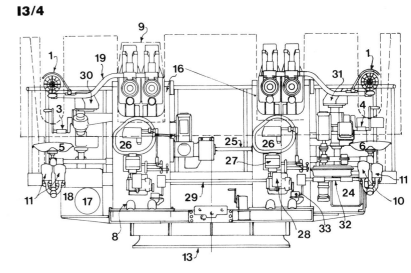

I3/5

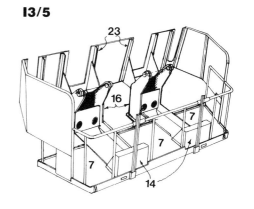

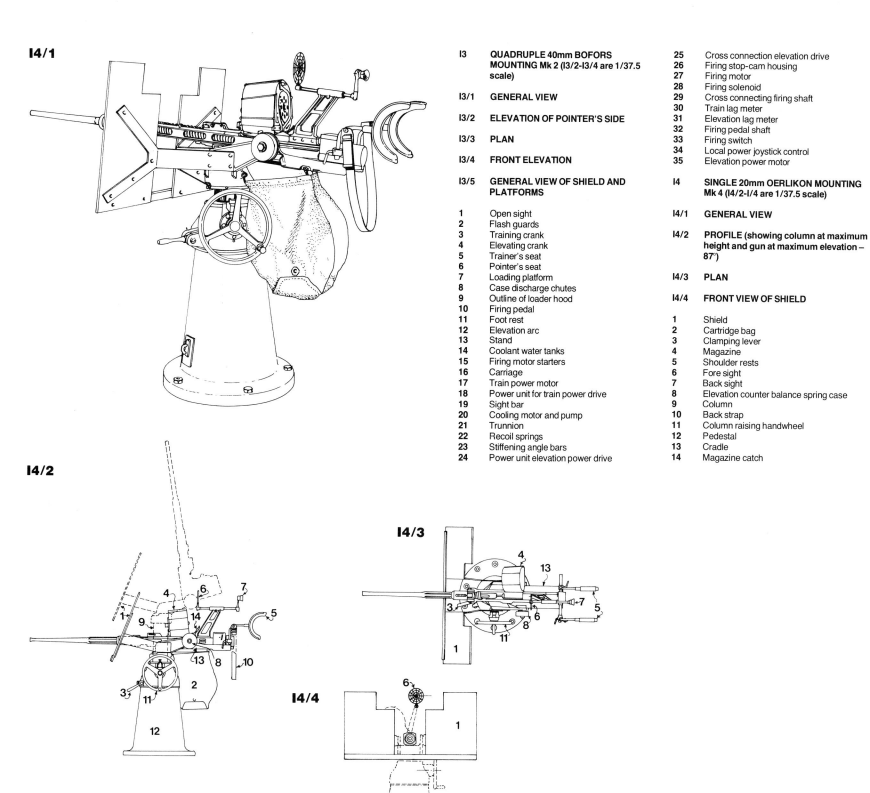

I4/1

I3	**QUADRUPLE 40mm BOFORS MOUNTING Mk 2 (I3/2-I3/4 are 1/37.5 scale)**		25	Cross connection elevation drive
			26	Firing stop-cam housing
I3/1	**GENERAL VIEW**		27	Firing motor
			28	Firing solenoid
I3/2	**ELEVATION OF POINTER'S SIDE**		29	Cross connecting firing shaft
			30	Train lag meter
I3/3	**PLAN**		31	Elevation lag meter
			32	Firing pedal shaft
I3/4	**FRONT ELEVATION**		33	Firing switch
			34	Local power joystick control
I3/5	**GENERAL VIEW OF SHIELD AND PLATFORMS**		35	Elevation power motor

1	Open sight		**I4**	**SINGLE 20mm OERLIKON MOUNTING Mk 4 (I4/2-I/4 are 1/37.5 scale)**
2	Flash guards			
3	Training crank		**I4/1**	**GENERAL VIEW**
4	Elevating crank			
5	Trainer's seat		**I4/2**	**PROFILE (showing column at maximum height and gun at maximum elevation – 87°)**
6	Pointer's seat			
7	Loading platform			
8	Case discharge chutes		**I4/3**	**PLAN**
9	Outline of loader hood			
10	Firing pedal		**I4/4**	**FRONT VIEW OF SHIELD**
11	Foot rest			
12	Elevation arc		1	Shield
13	Stand		2	Cartridge bag
14	Coolant water tanks		3	Clamping lever
15	Firing motor starters		4	Magazine
16	Carriage		5	Shoulder rests
17	Train power motor		6	Fore sight
18	Power unit for train power drive		7	Back sight
19	Sight bar		8	Elevation counter balance spring case
20	Cooling motor and pump		9	Column
21	Trunnion		10	Back strap
22	Recoil springs		11	Column raising handwheel
23	Stiffening angle bars		12	Pedestal
24	Power unit elevation power drive		13	Cradle
			14	Magazine catch

I4/2

I4/3

I4/4

▌ Armament

I5/1

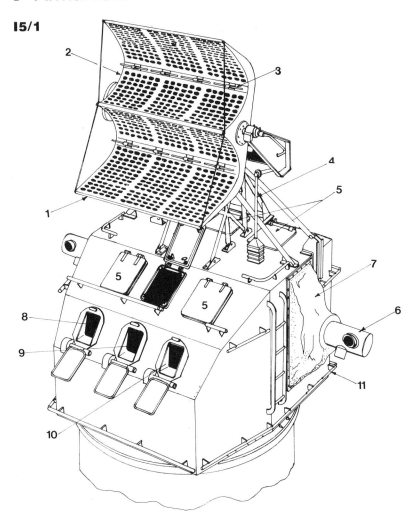

I5/3

I5/2

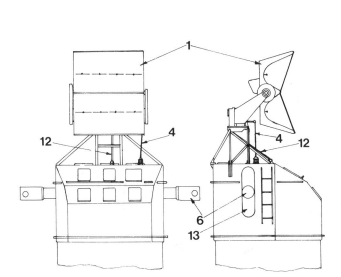

I5/4

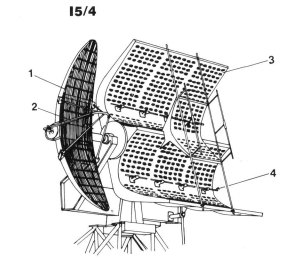

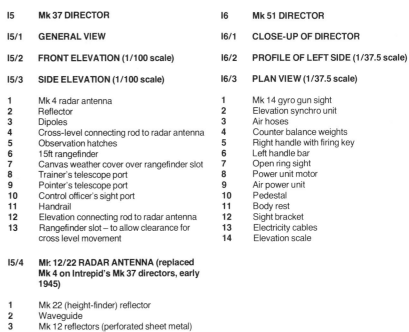

I6/1

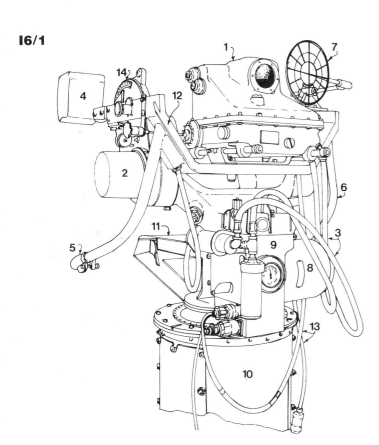

I6/2

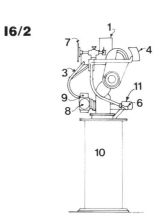

I6/3

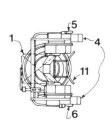

J Fittings

J1 GUARDRAILS (stanchions 1/37.5 scale, details enlarged)

These were of three basic types – permament, semi-permanent and removable. The former type consisted of fixed tubular stanchions with tubular guardrails welded to them, the semi-permanent had fixed stanchions with removable flexible steel wire lifelines while the last also had stanchions which could be hinged down. The lifelines were fitted in lengths with clips at each end and a bottle screw for adjusting length. In some positions chains were substituted for wire. Stanchion details were consistent but interchageable so there were considerable variations; the following examples cover all details but not all variations.

1 Standard lifeline stanchion with lifeline hooks and outboard screw-in fixing at heel
2 Braced stanchion with rings for fixing ends of lifelines and hinged heel fitted inboard
3 Flight deck stanchion for single lifeline (as fitted around elevator openings etc) with bayonet heel fixing in wood deck
4 Stanchion with lifeline rings and screw in heel at corner position
5 Detail plan of stanchion lifeline rings
6 Detail of stanchion brace lug

7 Detail of lifeline hooks fitted on intermediate stanchion
8 Detail of stanchion brace – the angled end bolted directly to the deck, however this was not consistent some being formed with flat ends for fixing to vertical surfaces. The length (arrowed) was normally 4ft 2in, and the standard stanchion height, from the deck, 3ft 8in
9 Bayonet heel fixing for flight deck
10 Corner screw-in heel fixing (plan view)
11 Bayonet heel fixing
12 Hinged heel fixing (the hook is a lifeline support for use with the stanchion hinged down)
13 Outboard screw-in heel fixing
14 Short lifeline stanchion as fitted at the top of low screens, etc
15 Angle bar stanchion, fitted on walkways and platforms around and under flight deck, holes for lifeline. Heel welded outboard
16 Braced angle walkway stanchion with ring strap for lifeline ends. Heels welded outboard
17 Guardrail stanchion with lifeline rings on one side. Heel welded outboard of deck edge
18 Standard guardrail stanchion. Heel welded inboard of deck edge
19 Section of angle bar stanchion showing lifeline ring strap
20 Clip fitted at ends of lifelines
21 Clip and bottle screw fitted at ends of lifelines (each lifeline had one end as 20 and one as 21)

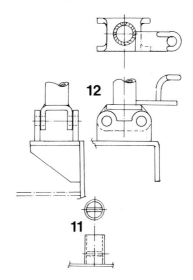

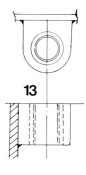

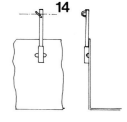

J1

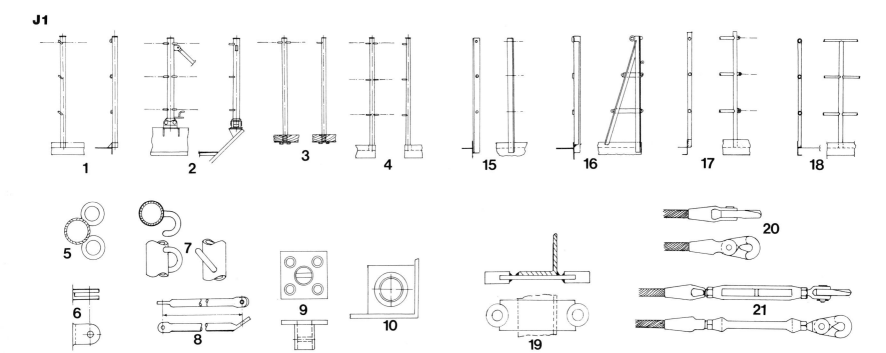

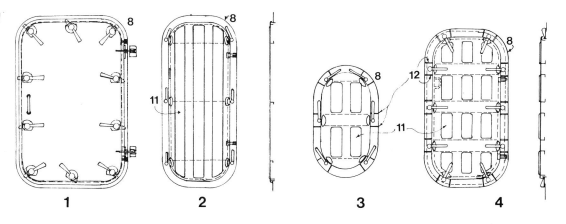

J2/1

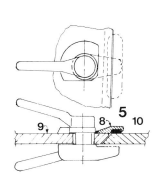
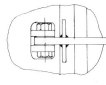
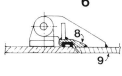
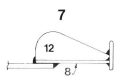

J2/2   QUICK-ACTING DOOR (these were similar to standard doors but were fitted with a mechanism which released all the dogs with one movement. This was particularly useful in positions where doors were in constant use but were required, for damage control or other purposes, to be kept closed as much as possible)

J2/2

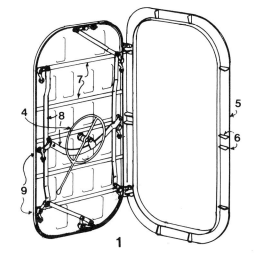

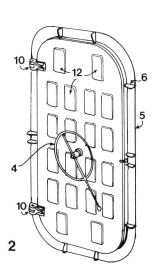

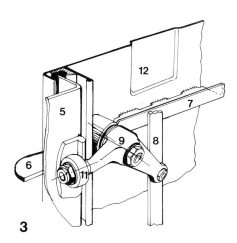

J Fittings

J3

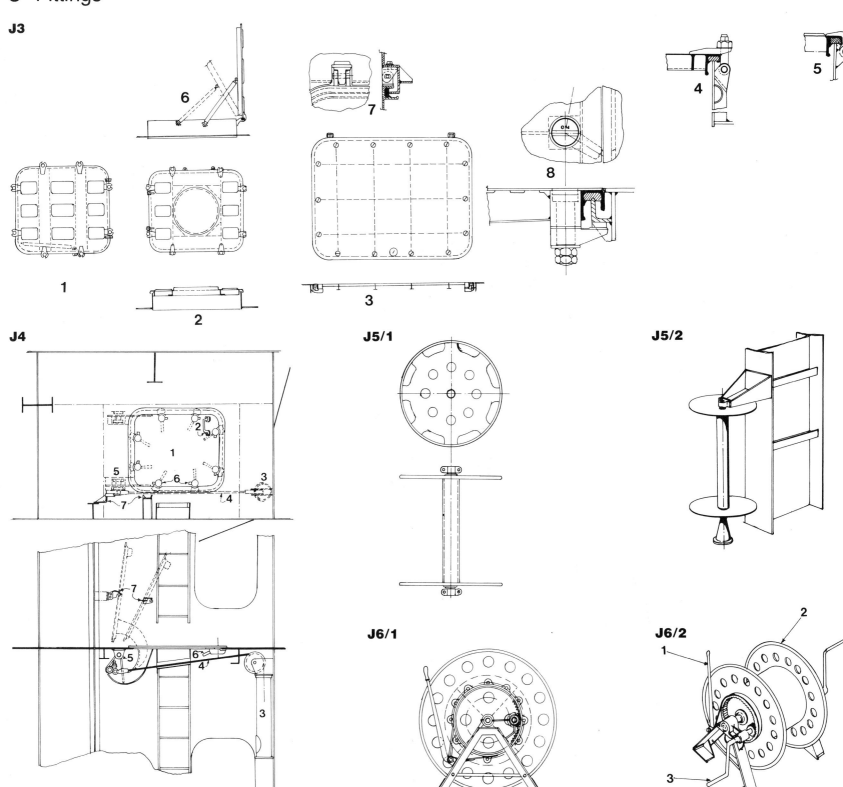

1

2

3

6

7

8

4

5

J4

1

2

3

4

5

6

7

J5/1

J5/2

J6/1

J6/2

1

2

3

J7

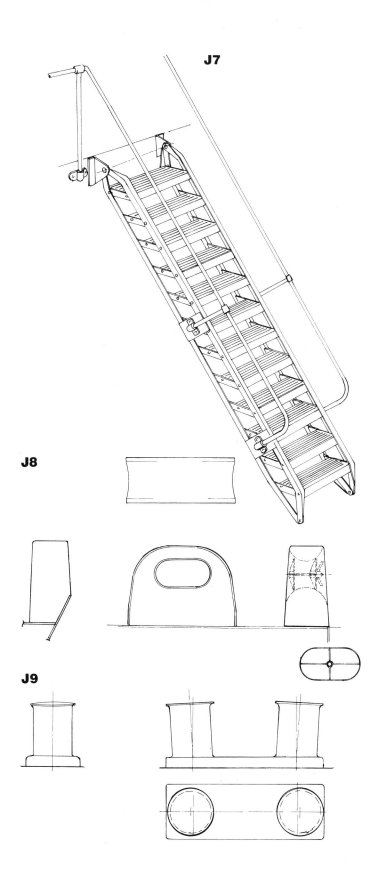

J8

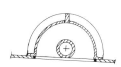

J9

J3 **TYPICAL HATCHWAYS (1/37.5 scale, details enlarged)**

1 Water-tight hatch
2 Water-tight hatch with escape manhole
3 Flush air-tight and fume-tight hatch
4 Detail of hatch dog
5 Detail of hatch hinge
6 Detail of hatch braces with alternative positions
7 Detail of hinge for flush hatch
8 Detail of clip for flush hatch

J4 **TYPICAL ARMOURED HATCH (1/37.5 scale)**

1 Hatch (same thickness as deck)
2 Lifting handle
3 Counter balance spring case
4 Counter balance cable
5 Hinge
6 Clips
7 Hatch retaining catch

J5/1 **TYPICAL MANILA ROPE HAWSER REEL (stowed both horizontally and vertically – brackets part of ship's structure. 1/37.5 scale)**

J5/2 **MANILLA ROPE REEL**

These were made in various lengths and fitted both vertically (as shown) and

horizontally (similar to wire rope reels). When raised off the deck or fitted horizontally, a bracket (shown at the top here) was fitted at both ends.

J6/1 **TYPICAL STEEL CABLE HAWSER REEL (with geared drive and brake. 1/37.5 scale)**

J6/2 **WIRE ROPE REEL**

1 Brake (one side only)
2 Round bar welded around rim
3 Crank (portable)

J7 **TYPICAL LADDER (constructed with angle bar runners and steps from flat sheets formed into upturned trays. Note: Hinged top fixing to lift ladder clear of deck and tubular steel hand rails. One flange of each of the angle bar runners is tapered off at both ends)**

J8 **FAIRLEAD (showing cover plate fitted in recess of those inside hangar to prevent entry of water in rough weather. 1/37.5 scale)**

J9 **BITT (1/37.5 scale)**

J10 **BLIND BITT (fitted in side plating just above waterline. 1/37.5 scale)**

J10

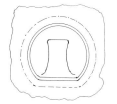

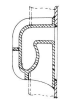

J Fittings

J11

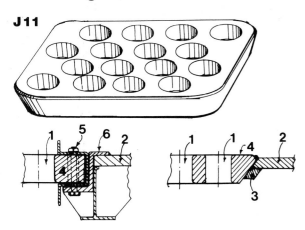

J11 **ARMOURED GRATING** (insets: sections at edge of gratings. These were fitted in all uptake and downtake openings in the main and 4th decks, the size, and hence number of holes varying to suit the position. That shown is the type used in air vents; for the funnel uptakes – where allowance had to be made for heat expansion – the gratings were fixed to the deck by means of bolts fitted through elongated holes as shown in the section at left)

1 Vent hole
2 STS deck
3 Holding block (welded)
4 4½in armour plate grating (welded into opening)
5 Bolt
6 Shelf welded to deck

J12 **PARAVANE GEAR** (1/300 scale)

1 Paravane boom
2 Boom guys
3 Overhead paravane transporting rail
4 Paravanes, stowed
5 Downhauler
6 Paravane towing wire
7 Paravane in position for release

J12

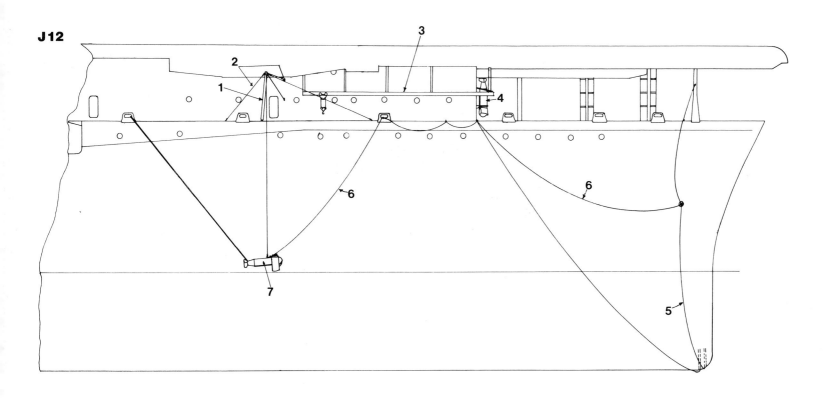

K Boats

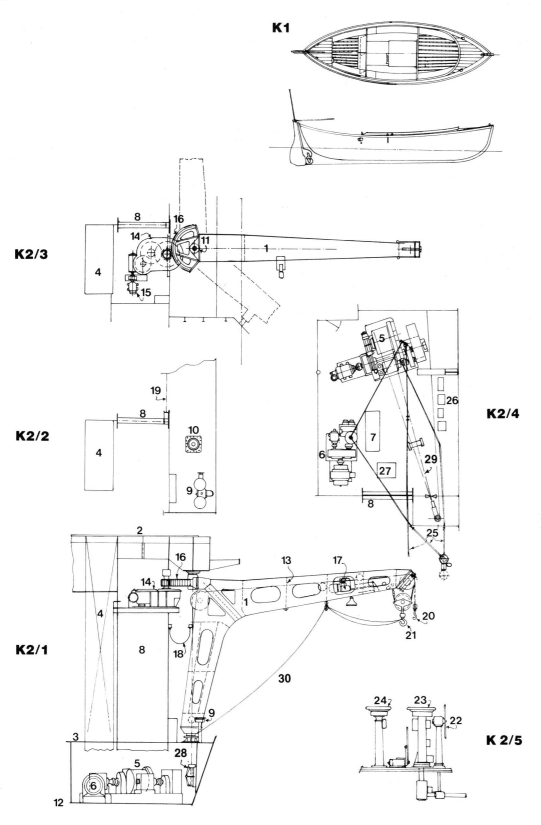

K1 **26ft MOTOR WHALEBOAT (1/150 scale)**

K1

K2/3

K2/2

K2/1

K2/4

K 2/5

K1	**26ft MOTOR WHALEBOAT (1/150 scale)**
K2	**BOAT AND AIRCRAFT CRANE (forward crane illustrated. K2/1-K2/4 1/150 scale, K2/5 1/75 scale)**
K2/1	**PROFILE WITH CRANE SWUNG OUTBOARD (looking forward)**
K2/2	**PLAN (at main deck)**
K2/3	**PLAN (at top of crane)**
K2/4	**PLAN OF CRANE MACHINERY (on 2nd deck)**
K2/5	**DETAIL OF CONTROLS (looking inboard)**

1	Jib (of rectangular cross section)
2	Flight deck
3	Main deck
4	Bomb elevator
5	Crane winch
6	Main power plant (electro-hydraulic)
7	Booster pump for power plant (fitted after completion)
8	Flight deck foundation girder
9	Crane controls
10	Lower bearing
11	Upper bearing
12	2nd deck
13	Frames on inside of jib
14	Training gear box
15	Training motor
16	Training pinion and arc (latter fixed to jib)
17	Paying out gear
18	Electric cable loop
19	Roller curtain
20	Aircraft lift hook
21	Main lift hook
22	Emergency brakes
23	Rotation control standard
24	Hoist control standard
25	Control rods from control position to machinery
26	Winch controls
27	Main motor control
28	Lift wire brake
29	Lifts run through centre of crane lower bearing
30	Safety runner

95

K Boats

K3

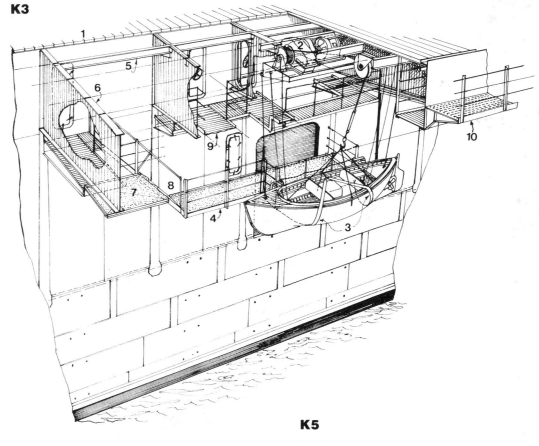

K5

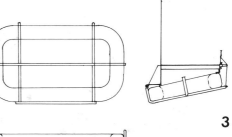

K4

K6

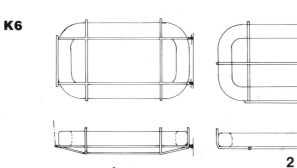